MW01173714

IN YOUR FACE

devil

TAKIN' BACK

MY STUFF

A survival manual

Syl Edwards

Revised and Expanded Edition

Copyright © 2008 by Syl Edwards

IN YOUR FACE devil TAKIN' BACK MY STUFF
A survival manual
by Syl Edwards

Printed in the United States of America

ISBN 978-1-60647-686-4

All rights reserved solely by the author. The author guarantees all contents are original and do not infringe upon the legal rights of any other person or work. No part of this book may be reproduced in any form without the permission of the author. The views expressed in this book are not necessarily those of the publisher.

Unless otherwise indicated, Bible quotations are taken from The King James Version of the Bible, and The Amplified Bible or The New King James Version, Copyright © 1987 by The Lockman Foundation.

The listing of "Who Am I?" is from an unknown author.

www.xulonpress.com

The purpose that God directed this book to be written is so that His people may learn who they are in Christ, that they may learn to stand against the devil, and reclaim for themselves and others, the things that the devil has stolen, that these things may be restored. A coordinating workbook is also available.

WITH GOD ALL THINGS ARE
POSSIBLE!

DEDICATION

This book is dedicated, first of all to my Lord and Savior Jesus Christ, to Whom I will forever be grateful that He died for me and that I was received into the family of God. He has shown me His healing power, spiritually, through His Word, and also physical and emotional healing. God has delivered me and healed me of the scars of life that for a great while, I didn't even know I had. This book is written, not out of MY ability, but rather "Not by might, nor by power, but by My Spirit," says the Lord of hosts". (Zechariah 4:6) Secondly, I give thanks to my loving husband, Fred Edwards. Without his patience and encouragement, the long hours he endured without me while I was preparing this book...it would never have been completed. He's a strong prayer warrior and my best friend and I can't thank God enough for putting him in my life. He's my greatest gift in life, since Jesus. Thirdly, to my mentor, Bishop Paul Crites, "Dr. Purpose" I give thanks for all his teaching, time and advice. Without his mentoring, I never ever would have thought that I could write a book. "How do you write a book?" He asked. "One chapter at a time." Through his mentoring, we "discovered our purpose", one for which God has been preparing us, probably all our lives.

TABLE OF CONTENTS

CHAPTER 1

****

WHO IS GOD?

****

Who is God? What's He all about? What's He like?

The NIV Compact Dictionary of the Bible published by Zondervan in 1999 defines God as:

> "A nonmaterial personal being, self-conscious and self-determining, He is everywhere, everything everywhere is immediately in His Presence. His omniscience is all-inclusive — He eternally knows what He has known in the past and what He will know in the future. His omnipotence is the ability to do with power all that power can do, controlling all the power that is or can be...God is eternal, without temporal beginning or ending...God is unchangeable. God is known supremely

through His Son (Hebrews 1:1 & 2). God is known by faith, in fellowship with His people (Hebrews 11:6)." Holiness is stated to be God's central ethical attribute. And I agree completely with this statement.

Many people have a concept of God as being high up in Heaven, an old man with a long white beard, who is just waiting up there for you to do something wrong, so He can "get ya". It's been instilled in many that God is to be feared. Well, yes, and no. Yes, we are to fear God. We are wise if we fear His punishment, deserved by each of us when we have not made our peace with Him through His Son, Jesus. You see, until we receive Jesus as our personal Savior from sin, we actually belong to the devil's family. (John 8:42-44) Once you receive Jesus as your Savior, once you receive His sacrifice on His death on the cross for yourself, then you become a part of the family of God (John 3:16).

Now, God becomes your Father. Judgment for sin is now gone and we are under His love and mercy. There are many Scriptures that show God as our Father:

Old Testament:

Deuteronomy 32:6; Psalm 68:5&6; Psalm 103:13; Isaiah 9:6; Isaiah 64:8; Malachi 2:10

New Testament:

Matthew 7:11; Matthew 23:9; Luke 11:2; John 1:14; 1 Corinthians 8:5, 6; Ephesians 4:6; Philippians 2:11; Hebrews 12:9; 1 Peter 1:17; Revelation 1:6

The Bible tells us that God IS love. (1 John 4: 7-10). So now the picture changes here. God always DID love you, you know? He knew you and loved you before you were a twinkle in your Momma's eye (Isaiah 44:2; Psalm 139:1-14; Jeremiah 1:5). He knew you and me when we were being formed inside our mother's womb. He knows us so intimately that He knows the number of hairs on our head. Matthew 10:30, Luke 12:7. Do you know that He knows YOUR name? Well, He does. Numbers 1:1-15 is a perfect example of this. God specifically named 11 men and appointed them to count those in their tribe. God knows your name. Incredible, isn't it???? And, He's always thinking about you. Psalm 139:17, 18; Psalm 40:17. Many of us have a poor father image from what we grew up with, or what we grew up without. We may have missed out on what a loving father should be. Our natural father may have rejected us and caused us emotional pain and torment. Maybe we don't even know who he is. God is not like that. God dearly dearly loves you and wants you to come to Him as His child. He will not force you to come. He will not force you to love Him. But, He loves you so much that in order for you to be in Heaven with Him one day, He sent His Son,

Jesus, to die for you. Jesus also loves you so much, that He came here to earth from Heaven, just to die on the cross for YOU. Do you know anybody who would be willing to die for you? I sure don't. Yes, there are occasional people who will pay the ultimate sacrifice for another. But they are sinful people, like us, and they could not die to give you eternal life. Only sinless Jesus could do that for us. Don't think you're a sinner? I didn't either. I figured that since I didn't kill anyone or rob a bank or anything serious like that, that I was a good person. Not so! Friends, we're BORN with sin. Many times the first word we learn to say is "NO". Psalm 58:3

It's been said that each of us has a God shaped "hole" within us, that only God can fill. This is true. If money and fame could make us happy like many of us think, then why are all those Hollywood personalities overdosing on drugs and marrying and divorcing like we change our underwear? They're not happy. No husband, wife or children can create joy in your life. They may help create happiness, but not inner joy. No human being can do that. Knowing God is the only way to stop the emptiness you feel within.

We need to respect and honor God. God has done so many things in my life and I've come to know Him better over the years. This is an individual thing too. We have to make the effort to get to know God. He already knows us. We had to get to know our natural daddy too, what pleases him, what displeases him. We run to our parents for protection, for love, for comfort, when we need something. As children, we don't stop and wonder if it's OK to approach them. We just barge in and make our needs known and expect them to be met. God is going to fill your needs. Did you know that you're the "apple" of God's eye? (Deuteronomy 32: 9-10) Well, you are.

God is loving, but God is also holy and just. He needs to be treated and approached with utmost respect and reverential fear.

In Leviticus 10:1-11, Nadab and Abihu, Aaron's sons were killed by God for improper irreverent service to Him. They were authorized to come before Him in service to Him, but they came irreverently. They failed to acknowledge His holiness. They failed to reverence and fear Him. On the other hand, Abraham immediately obeyed God and set about to go sacrifice his cherished son, Isaac.

In Acts 5, Ananias & Saphira, husband and wife had sold a piece of property and they decided between themselves not to give the entire proceeds as a contribution to the church. They could have given just a portion or part of the sale and that would have been fine. They decided to lie and have it appear that they were giving the whole sum of money. God struck them dead! He cannot tolerate sin. After we receive Jesus as our Savior, we do not become perfect. Only our spirit person has been made brand new. Our soul part is still very human and we have to control it and bring it into alignment with the Word of God. As you come to know God and to love Him, you will not want to hurt or offend Him in any way at all.

In Mark 12:28-31 Jesus tells us to love God with our whole heart, all of our soul and our entire mind and with all our strength. You're going to WANT to please Him. So when you "blow it", and you will at some point, stop, turn away from that sin, ask God to forgive you, and He will. (1 John 1:7-10)

You will find no greater joy than having a personal relationship with God through Jesus Christ. God's love for you is Unfailing (Psalm 33). People will fail you, but God never will. Everlasting (Jeremiah 31:3); Abounding (Psalm 86:5), always available to give you mercy; God, Himself, is love. (1 John 4:8). God's heart is filled with pain because He loves people who don't love Him back.

In Luke 15:11-24 we find the account of the prodigal son. The younger son boldly asks his father for his share of the inheritance he would receive upon the father's death. I don't know why, but the father gave it to him. If it were me, I would have just told my son to "get lost", that he'd have to wait till the proper time. But the father gave this son his inheritance and the son promptly went off, out of the county, and proceeded to spend all he had on wine, women and song. He partied big time. No doubt he had lots of friends, till the money ran out. Then his "friends" deserted him and he had to go to work to live. He ended up taking care of pigs which were unclean, animals that in his religion, he was not even to touch. No one helped him out. One day, the Word says, he "came to his senses", and realized how bad off he was, how even the servants in his father's house were better off than he. He realized his sin and offense against his father and decided to go home and ask forgiveness of his father so that he could just live there, just like a hired man. But you know what?

His father, full of love for his missing son had been looking for him to return home every day. Every day he was out searching the horizon, hoping to see his son returning home. One day his horizon searching paid off and in the distance he saw a speck in the distance. His heart leaped for joy and excitement. He just KNEW it was his son!!!!! He ran to meet his son, hugging and kissing him when they met. It must have been a tearful reunion. The young man got part of his apology speech out. But, his father interrupted it by commanding that the best robe (his own probably) be brought and put on his son and a ring for his hand and sandals for his feet, and he directed that the calf who had been fed in preparation for a feast be brought out and killed so that they could celebrate the son's return home. What a joyful time!

You know friends, this is a picture of God...and you. God wants you to return to Him. He wants to reinstate you as His child. You've been away from Him for much too long. Come back to Him. Come back to Him now. There's NOTHING you could have possibly done for which He will not forgive you. He loves you so much. Talk to Him from your heart. God won't turn you away. He's been looking for you, waiting for you. Come back to Him now.

Did you know that God still speaks to us today? Well, He does. We just need to know how to listen.

GOD CAN SPEAK TO US

In an audible voice (one which we can actually hear). Matthew 3:17, Acts 9:3-4

Through reading His Word. Psalm 119:105
His Spirit to our spirit. Romans 8:17
Through gifts of the Spirit. 1 Corinthians 12:7-11
Through His Prophets. Hebrews 1:1-2, Acts 13:1-2
Through counsel with people. Proverbs 11:14
Through angels. Matthew 1:20
Through dreams. Matthew 1:20, Matthew 2:12
Through visions. Acts 10:3-4. Acts 10:9, 10, 17
Through circumstances. Jeremiah 32:7-9

These points were gleaned from a Bible study lesson given by Dennis Evensen, Pastor of World Outreach Church of God in Patchogue, New York, some years ago, and still relevant today. Some things never change.

Guidance from God does not come automatically. James 3:15-17. We need to seek God's guidance. Receiving guidance from God is a skill to be learned. There isn't a "method". It's a personal thing, like going to your Dad or Mom to ask their advice, only better. Many times guidance happens when we don't know it, when we're not looking for it, when we're moving in life, "as we're going".

We need to pray for God's guidance as we have our daily prayer time with God. Did you notice I said "daily" prayer with God? This is the key, to have a life drenched in prayer. My husband is a prayer warrior. I've never known anyone who prays as much as Fred does. He prays over EVERYTHING....and this is how it should be. I learn lots from him in this regard.

OUR GOD IS THE GOD OF THE IMPOSSIBLE

The account of Moses is classic example of this fact, found starting in Exodus, chapter 2. Moses was the son of Amram and Jochebed. Both of them were from the Tribe of Levi. Now Pharaoh had commanded that all Hebrew male children be thrown into the river after birth, to kill them. Moses' parents hid him for 3 months, and then his mother built an ark or basket for him, put Moses in it and laid it among the bulrushes at the edge of the Nile River. Miriam, his sister, set herself to watch what would happen. They expected God to do something. Because GOD IS THE GOD OF THE IMPOSSIBLE.

Pharoah's daughter found the baby and called him Moses and raised him as a prince, paying Moses' natural mother to be a nursemaid to Moses. OUR GOD IS THE GOD OF THE IMPOSSIBLE!

After Moses was a grown man, he tried to take matters of injustice into his own hands and he killed an Egyptian who was beating a Hebrew. Moses fled from Pharoah's presence into the land of Midian, where he met his wife and started a family, tending to his father-in-law's flocks. In Exodus 3 we find that it was in Midian that God appeared to Moses from the middle of a burning bush....a bush on fire but not being consumed by the flames—OUR GOD IS THE GOD OF THE IMPOSSIBLE!

God told Moses He had seen and heard of the afflictions of the Hebrew people and that He had come to deliver them, through Moses. Moses suddenly got a case of fear and trembling, making excuses to God why he couldn't be used. God answered each of Moses' obstacles, telling Moses to go to the elders of the Hebrews and tell them God had heard their cry and was going to free them from bondage. God told Moses to go to the King of Egypt and tell him that the Lord, the God of the Hebrews said "Let My people go." God told Moses Pharoah would not agree and that He would do mighty wonders. OUR GOD IS THE GOD OF THE IMPOSSIBLE!

In Exodus 4 we see Moses telling God to "send someone else". Then God got angry with Moses. You need to read this yourself. The end result here is that Aaron, Moses' brother, would be the voice to Pharoah, using the words that Moses was to give him, and Moses was to speak as God to Aaron. Moses was to use the rod for the signs, but it turned out that not only did Aaron speak the words given to Moses by God, but Aaron ALSO did the signs with the rod (Exodus 4:30). OUR GOD IS THE GOD OF THE IMPOSSIBLE!...even when we're unwilling.

In the course of time, God did many signs before Pharoah and the people of Egypt and it seemed to only get worse for the Hebrew people.

The signs God did:

1) Aaron's rod became a serpent.
2) The waters of Egypt became blood, in all the bodies of water and even in all the containers.

The fish in the river died and began to stink and the water began to stink.

3) Frogs came and were into EVERYTHING.

4) All the dust of the land became biting gnats or mosquitoes in all the land. After this plague Pharoah's magicians believed this was God.

5) Swarms of bloodsucking gadflies came into the house of Pharoah and his servants, and the land was ruined by these insects. But none of this happened in the land of the Hebrews. All the livestock of Egypt that were out in the fields died. But, not one of the Hebrews' livestock died.

6) Boils and sores were put on man and beasts on all the land occupied by the Egyptians.

7) Hail, heavy and dreadful, ran down and along the ground, fire with thunder and lightning continually.

8) Some of Pharoah's people believed it was coming and took their people and animals inside. Everyone and everything left outside suffered the consequences. Only in Goshen, where the Israelites were, there was no hail.

9) Locusts came and ate the remainder of the crops and trees that the hail had not gotten, and they filled the houses of all the Egyptians. And lastly,

10) The first born of everyone and everything in all the land of Egypt died, including Pharoah's son. Then Pharoah let the Hebrew people go out of his land and they left Egypt rich

people. OUR GOD IS THE GOD OF THE IMPOSSIBLE!

Then, Pharoah changed his mind AGAIN, and began to pursue the Hebrews and they cornered them at the Red Sea. BUT GOD opened the sea. He parted the waters so that the Hebrews crossed on DRY land with two high walls of water on either side of them. I understand that there were 2 million people in that group of people, so that the area they crossed over in would have had to be four miles wide to accommodate all of them. What a sight that must have been!!!! The Hebrews went through and Pharoah and men went in after them. The God caused the sea to return to its strength and normal flow and Pharoah and his army and chariots and horses all were drowned.

Exodus 15:2-3 tells me that the Lord is my strength and my song…the Lord is a Man of War and The Lord is His Name. OUR GOD IS THE GOD OF THE IMPOSSIBLE!

Whatever we're going through in life, we need to stand firm and trust in our God. Have faith in Him. Believe His Word.

He doesn't fail. The circumstances of life may try to tie you up and throw you into an emotional fire, or a physical one. But, we have within us the Greater, the Mightier One. GREATER, GREATER, GREATER is He that is within us than he that is in the world. No one else can deliver us out of the fires of life……NO ONE.

God is with us in the fire, and He'll walk us THROUGH THE FIRE, and He'll walk us OUT OF

THE FIRE! We have El Shaddai with us, the God who is MORE than enough.

Hebrews 11:6 says "But without faith it is impossible to please and be satisfactory to Him, for whoever would come near to God must necessarily believe that God exists and that He is the Rewarder of those who earnestly and diligently seek Him out."

What does <u>GOD</u> say about Himself?

Exodus 34:5 & 6: "Then the Lord came down in a pillar of cloud and called out His own Name "The Lord". As Moses stood there in His Presence He passed in front of Moses and said "I am the Lord, I am the Lord, the merciful and gracious God."

Nehemiah 9:5: "Stand up and praise the Lord your God, for He lives from everlasting to everlasting." PRAISE HIS GLORIOUS NAME!

Exodus 15:2: "The Lord is my strength and my song. He has become my victory. He is my God and I will praise Him. He is my father's God and I will exalt Him." GOD IS OUR VERY STRENGTH AND VICTORY.

Deuteronomy 10:21: "He is the one who is worthy of your praise, the one Who has done mighty miracles that you yourselves have seen." We need to think about all the miracles God has done in our life.

Psalm 146:10: 'The Lord will reign forever. O Jerusalem, your God is King is every generation! Praise the Lord!" God is King and Ruler of all!

Micah 7: 18: "Where is another God like You Who pardons the sins of the survivors among His people? You cannot stay angry with Your people forever because You delight in showing mercy." God forgives our sins and delights in showing us mercy

Psalm 140:7 "Sovereign Lord, my strong Savior, You protected me on the day of battle." He's our strong Savior. He protects me.

Acts 4:24: "Then all the believers were united as they lifted their voices in prayer — "Oh, Sovereign Lord, Creator of heaven and earth, the sea and everything in them." He created heaven and earth, the sea and everything in them.

Romans 8:15 & 16: "So you should not be like cowering, fearful slaves. You should behave instead like God's very own children calling Him "Father, dear Father", for His Holy Spirit speaks to us deep in our hearts and tells us that we are God's children." God loves us and wants us to return to Him as His children. He doesn't want us to cower before ANYTHING.

Romans 6:23: "For the wages of sin is death, but the wages of sin is death, but the free gift of God is eternal life through Christ Jesus Our Lord." By God's mercy, ALL can be released from death.

Psalm 48:10: "As Your Name deserves, Oh God, You will be praised to the ends of the earth. Your strong right hand is filled with victory." Even in our darkest hour, we can have faith in God's ultimate victory.

Romans 8:38 & 39: "And I am convinced that nothing can ever separate us fro His love –death can't and life can't – our fears for today, our worries about tomorrow and even the powers of hell can't keep God's love away—nothing in all creation will ever be able to separate us from the love of God that is revealed in Christ Jesus." Nothing can ever separate us from God's love. God's love is stronger than ANY other power in the universe.

Genesis 14:20: "And blessed be God most high Who has helped you conquer your enemies." God is our <u>EVER</u> present help... Even in the midst of trouble, we can have God's peace, through His grace.

Romans 16:20: "The God of peace will soon crush satan under your feet." God gives us the peace that can surpass all human understanding.

Psalm 144:2: "He is my loving ally and my fortress, my tower of safety, my deliverer— He stands before me as a shield and I take refuge in Him. He subdues the nations under me." God is my place of safety. He fights for me and in Him I can be victorious in all things.

Psalm 24:8: "Who is the King of Glory? The Lord, strong and mighty."

Joshua 2:11: "The Lord your God is the Supreme God of the heavens above and the earth below." There is no one more powerful than our God!

Psalm 7:17: "I will thank the Lord because He is just." God is fair and He understands ALL things.

Isaiah 26:4: "Trust in the Lord always for the Lord God is the eternal rock." No matter what storms come our way, we're always safe with God. He is always here for us.

Isaiah 40:28: "Have you never heard or understood? Don't you know that the Lord is the Everlasting God, the Creator of all the earth? He never grows faint or weary. No one can measure the depths of His understanding." Trust in the God of all creation. His strength will never fail you. He never gets tired. He never sleeps.

Psalm 31:5: "I entrust my spirit into Your Hand. Rescue me Lord for You are a faithful God." God is completely trustworthy and will never fail us. He will always provide for us.

1 John 4:16: "We know how much God loves us and we have put our trust in Him. God is love and all who live in love live in God and God lives in them." God really, really, really loves you.

Psalm 23:1: "The Lord is my Shepherd—I have everything I need." All my needs are met in God.

Psalm 40:17: "As for me, I am poor and needy, but the Lord is thinking about me right now." I'm always on God's mind.

Psalm 147:3: "He heals the broken hearted, binding up their wounds." God heals emotional, as well as physical needs. God feels and understands my pain.

Malachi 4:2: "But you who fear My Name, the sun of Righteousness will rise with healing in His wings, and you shall go free, leaping with joy like calves let out to pasture." God sets us free from our burdens and gives us joy. He sent Jesus so that through Him, we'd receive our healing.

God forgives our sins and delights in mercy and loving kindness. Micah 7:19/Psalm 103:3 & 12.

He is wiser than men and the weak thing of God is stronger than men. I Corinthians 1:24. His strength and power are made perfect and show themselves most effective in our weaknesses. II Corinthians 12:9. God's Grace is more than enough for us. God chose you and me, even the things that are nothing. God can use even me! 1 Corinthians 1:28. And, because of our faith in Christ, we can dare to have the boldness of free access to God, without fear. Ephesians 3:12.

God will always have time for you. He always has time to hear your prayers and to care about you. He's said that He will never leave us or fail us in any way. Joshua 1:5/ Hebrews 13:5/ Psalm 139:1-6. God knows everything about us and all that we are doing. Nothing takes God by surprise. He never goes "Oops" or "Uh Oh!"

God is merciful. No matter how you "blow it", God is always right there waiting to forgive you. We have no need to fear Him. What we need to do is to RUN TO Him. He will never desert those who seek Him. Psalm 9:10.

NAMES OF GOD

ELOHIM: MIGHTY, THE STRONG ONE, THE SUPREME GOD

ADONAI: MASTER, LORD, OWNER OF EVERYTHING, SOVEREIGN LORD

JEHOVAH JIREH: PROVIDES FOR US

JEHOVAH ROPHE: HEALER

EL SHADDAI: ALL MIGHTY, NURTURES, SUSTAINS, THE GOD WHO IS MORE THAN ENOUGH

JEHOVAH SHALOM: JEHOVAH IS PEACE

JEHOVAH SHAMMAH: JEHOVAH IS THERE, IN THE PRESENT, HERE AND NOW.

JEHOVAH NISSI: JEHOVAH IS MY BANNER

JEHOVAH ROHI/JEHOVAH RAF: JEHOVAH IS MY SHEPHERD

JEHOVAH TSID KENU:OUR RIGHTEOUSNESS

JEHOVAH M'KADDESH: WHO SANCTIFIES

EL OLAM: EVERLASTING ONE

EL ELYON: GOD MOST HIGH, STRONGEST STRONG ONE

EL ELHOE ISRAEL: THE LORD GOD OF ISRAEL

JEHOVAH RAAH: MY SHEPHERD

EL: GOD

YAHWEH: ETERNAL CREATOR, COVENANT KEEPER, THE LORD

THE LIFE EVERLASTING

THE LORD, STRONG AND MIGHTY

KING ABOVE ALL THE EARTH

THE LORD GOD OF HOSTS

THE LORD GOD JEHOVAH

THE ONE WHO SUSTAINS ALL THINGS BY THE WORD OF HIS POWER

CHAPTER 2

****

THE NAME OF JESUS

****

I know you know the story of Jesus and His birth. But maybe you're like most folks who think Jesus was poor. Mary and Joseph weren't poor. They didn't plan for Jesus to be born in an animal shelter. They went to the local hotels. The hotels had no room for them. Mary couldn't give birth to Jesus on the street. Women gave birth to their children at home back then. Jesus wasn't poor as an adult either. In comparison to His heavenly home, yes He was. Earth is poor in comparison to Heaven. (2 Corinthians 8:9; John 10:10) Jesus wasn't the only Child of Mary. Mary and Joseph had children together. Luke 2:7 tells us that Mary gave birth to her first born. That alone tells us that others followed. Mark 6:1-3; Matthew 12:46-50, Matthew 13:55 & 56; Mark 3:31-35. Only Jesus' Father was God. The other children's father was

Joseph. The Baby, Mary's Son, the Son of God, was given the Name Jesus. In the Greek Jesus is Joshua, meaning Savior. In the Hebrew its Emmanuel, Immanuel, meaning God with us. Matthew 1:21 & 23, Isaiah 7:14. Jesus' natural birth Father is God. Matthew 1:18, Isaiah 9:6, Jeremiah 31:22, Micah 5:3-5; Matthew 1:18 & 23.

Another thing, the wise men...and we really don't know how many there were...didn't see Jesus as a brand new baby at the manger. They saw Him as a young child in a house, probably in Nazareth. Luke 2:1-17, Matthew 2:1-23. These verses all refer to "the young child". Joseph took "the child" and with Mary they fled to Egypt. King Herod had put to death all male children in Bethlehem ages 2 and younger.

Jesus' purpose being here on earth was to obey His Father. He came to earth purposely to die on the cross for us and to reunite us to His Father. In Luke 2, He already knew His purpose as a 12 year old child when He stayed behind in Jerusalem and Joseph and Mary were worried sick about Him. He was already "about His Father's business". Later, at 30 years old in the temple, Luke 3:23, He declared His purpose in front of all who were present there at the time. Luke 4:16-21, He came to earth to bring us complete salvation, spirit, soul and body, destroying the works of the devil. 1 John 3:8

Jesus lived a sinless life while He was here on earth. The Bible tells us that He was tempted is all ways like us, yet He didn't sin. Hebrews 4:15. Since He was tempted in ALL ways, He's able to under-stand our weaknesses and infirmities and challenges with temptation. He's able to save completely all who come to God through Him because He is alive forever and can continually petition God in our behalf. Hebrews 7:23. As a human being on earth, Jesus experienced human emotions, just like us. He was tired, impatient, sorrowful, appreciative, loving, and he got angry. John 2:13-17, 4:67, 6:26-27, 8:44, 11:35, 12:7 & 27, 13:1, 18:8 & 23.

Jesus is coming back again. He's not the tiny infant born in Bethlehem. Jesus is no longer the bloodied and badly beaten man crucified on a cross at Calvary. He's no longer just the risen dead man. Jesus is the King of Kings and Lord of Lords! Hallelujah! Glory to the Lamb of God!

NAMES OF JESUS

1. JESUS CHRIST, THE SON OF GOD
2. JESUS, THE ONE WHO SAVES MEN FROM THEIR SINS
3. THE CHRIST – THE ANOINTED ONE
4. THE ALPHA AND OMEGA, THE BEGINNING AND THE END
5. THE AUTHOR AND FINISHER OF OUR FAITH
6. EMMANUEL – GOD WITH US
7. THE CAPTAIN OF THE HOST
8. FAITHFUL AND TRUE
9. THE BREAD OF LIFE
10. THE LIVING WATERS
11. THE LIGHT OF THE WORLD
12. THE BRANCH

13. THE TRUE VINE
14. THE ROOT AND OFFSPRING OF DAVID
15. THE GOOD SHEPHERD
16. THE LAMB OF GOD
17. THE LAMB WITHOUT BLEMISH
18. THE LION OF THE TRIBE OF JUDAH
19. THE FULLNESS OF DEITY
20. MESSIAH, THE KING
21. THE HIGH PRIEST
22. THE HOLY ONE OF ISRAEL
23. THE LIVING WORD
24. THE LORD OF THE SABBATH
25. THE ROSE OF SHARON
26. THE LILY OF THE VALLEY
27. THE BRIGHT AND MORNING STAR
28. THE FAIREST OF TEN THOUSAND
29. THE FRIEND THAT STICKS CLOSER THAN
    A BROTHER
30. THE RESURRECTION AND THE LIFE
31. THE ROCK OF OUR SALVATION
32. THE CHIEF CORNERSTONE
33. THE SHEPHERD AND BISHOP OF SOULS
34. THE SON OF GOD
35. THE SON OF MAN
36. THE WORD MADE FLESH
37. THE WAY, THE TRUTH AND THE LIFE
38. WONDERFUL
39. COUNSELOR
40. THE MIGHTY GOD
41. THE EVERLASTING FATHER
42. THE PRINCE OF PEACE
43. THE KING OF KINGS

44. OUR CREATOR
45. OUR MESSIAH
46. OUR REDEEMER
47. OUR SAVIOR
48. OUR ROCK
49. OUR STRENGTH
50. OUR GOODNESS
51. OUR FORTRESS
52. OUR HIGH TOWER
53. OUR DELIVERER
54. OUR SHIELD
55. OUR BUCKLER
56. OUR TRUTH
57. OUR RIGHTEOUSNESS
58. OUR SALVATION
59. OUR FAITH
60. OUR KING
61. OUR MASTER
62. OUR LIFE
63. OUR LOVE

NAMES, TITLES AND DESCRIPTIONS OF JESUS IN THE BOOK OF HEBREWS

1:2	HEIR
1:2	LAWFUL OWNER OF ALL THINGS
1:3	SOLE EXPRESSION OF THE GLORY OF GOD
1:3	PERFECT IMPRINT AND VERY IMAGE OF GOD'S NATURE.
1:4	SUPERIOR TO ANGELS

1:5	GOD CALLS HIM "MY SON"
1:6	FIRSTBORN SON
1:8	GOD CALLS HIM "GOD"
1:10	GOD CALLS HIM "LORD"
1:12	YOU REMAIN THE SAME
2:6	SON OF MAN
2:7	CROWNED WITH GLORY AND HONOR AND SET HIM OVER THE WORKS OF YOUR HANDS
2:10	PIONEER OF OUR SALVATION
2:17	HIGH PRIEST
3:1	THE APOSTLE
3:1	HIGH PRIEST
3:2	FAITHFUL
3:4	BUILDER OF ALL THINGS
3:9	AUTHOR AND SOURCE OF ETERNAL SALVATION
3:10	HIGH PRIEST OF THE ORDER OF MELCHIZEDEK
6:20	FORERUNNER
7:22	THE GUARANTEE OF A BETTER AGREEMENT
8:2	MINISTER IN THE HOLY PLACES
8:6	MEDIATOR
8:2	OFFICIATING PRIEST
9:10	THE MESSIAH
9:15	THE NEGOTIATOR AND MEDIATOR OF A NEW AGREEMENT
12:2	THE LEADER
12:2	SOURCE OF OUR FAITH
12:2	FINISHER OF OUR FAITH

13:8   JESUS CHRIST, THE SAME, YESTERDAY,
        TODAY AND FOREVER
13:20   GREAT SHEPHERD OF THE SHEEP

The Word of God says that Jesus was given the most excellent name in heaven, earth and the world to come. It is even greater than any Name any where. Hebrews 1:1-4. He is the sole expression of the glory of God. He is mightier and superior to all angels. He is different and more perfect than them. He's the perfect image of God. He has God's personality and nature. He controls the working of our physical universe. He accomplished this not by His death, but by His resurrection after He offered Himself for our sins and guilt. Then He sat down at the right Hand of God and became as the Lord of Lords. Jesus is the power of God and the wisdom of God. 1 Corinthians 1:24.

PROPHECIES CONCERNING JESUS
(Thanks to Edward Hindson for his research)

    1. Born of a woman (Genesis 3:15)
    2. Born of a virgin (Isaiah 7:14)
    3. Son of God (Psalm 2:7)
    4. Seed of Abraham (Genesis 12:2-3)
    5. Seed of Isaac (Genesis 17:19)
    6. Son of Jacob (Numbers 24:17)
    7. Tribe of Judah (Genesis 49:10)
    8. Line of David (Isaiah 9:6-7)
    9. Born in Bethlehem (Micah 5:2)
    10. Prophet (Psalm 110:4)

11. Priest (Psalm 110:4)
12. King (Isaiah 9:7)
13. Anointed with the Holy Spirit (Isaiah 11:2)
14. Ministry in Galilee (Isaiah 9:1)
15. Miracles (Isaiah 35:5-6)
16. Enters the temple (Malachi 3:1)
17. Stumbling stone to the Jews (Psalm 118:22)
18. Light to the Gentiles (that's US) (Isaiah 42:6-7)
19. Betrayed for 30 pieces of silver (Zechariah 11:12)
20. Forsaken by His own followers (Zechariah 13:7)
21. Beaten and spit upon (Isaiah 50:6)
22 Publicly mocked (Psalm 22:7-8)
23 Cast lots for His garments (Psalm 22:7-8)
24 Crucified (Psalm 22:16, Zechariah 12:10)

"Psalm 22 mentions a lot of the specifics of what Jesus' death would be like. Verse 16 says, "...They pierced My hands and My feet..." referring to how Jesus was nailed to the cross. Verse 17 says two things: "I can count all My bones..." refers to the fact that they did not break Jesus' legs when they broke the other two prisoner's legs because he was already dead. It also says, "...They look and stare at Me," which refers to Him being put up on the cross and being publicly executed. Verse 18 says, "They divide My garments among them, and for My clothing they cast lots." That refers to the soldiers who executed Jesus diving up his garments and then casting lots for the fine robe that was put on him when he was given to the soldiers to be mocked and beaten. Verse 14 says, "I am poured out like water..." When the soldiers went to break the prisoner's legs so they would die faster, they discovered Jesus was already dead, so they thrust a spear in His side, and blood and water flowed out. You need to see the film "The Passion of the Christ" for a more vivid picture of what the crucifixion was probably like. Only, they didn't go far enough. Jesus was actually naked when he was beaten and crucified. Psalm 22 was written by King David thousands of years before Jesus was even born. The torture of crucifixion had not even been invented at the time when David wrote this."

This information was shared by Teresa Seputis via an email received August 2007.

25 Executed with criminals (Isaiah 53:12)
26 Buried with the rich (Isaiah 53:9)
27 Rise from the dead (Psalm 16:10)

Here's a fascinating article that I found on the internet, author not recorded by me:

Why did Jesus fold the linen cloth after His resurrection?

The Gospel of John (20: 7) tells us that the napkin, which was placed over the face of Jesus, was not just thrown aside like the grave clothes. The Bible takes an entire verse to tell us that the napkin was neatly folded, and was placed at the head of that stony coffin. Is that important? You'd better believe it! Is that significant? Absolutely! Is it really significant? Yes!

In order to understand the significance of the folded napkin, you have to understand a little bit about Hebrew tradition of that day. The folded napkin had to do with the Master and Servant, and every Jewish boy knew this tradition. When the servant set the dinner table for the master, he made sure that it was exactly the way the master wanted it. The table was furnished perfectly, and then the servant would wait, just out of sight, until the master had finished eating, and the servant would not dare touch that table, until the master was finished.

Now if the master was done eating, he would rise from the table, wipe his fingers, his mouth, and clean his beard, and would wad up that napkin and toss it onto the table. The servant would then know to clear the table. For in those days, the wadded napkin meant, "I'm done". But if the master got up from the table, and folded his napkin, and laid it beside his plate, the servant would not dare touch the table, because the servant knew that the folded napkin meant, "I'm not finished yet." The folded napkin meant, "I'm coming back!"

28 Ascends back to heaven (Psalm 16:10)
29 Seated at the right hand of God (Psalm 110:1)
30 Coming again (Zechariah 14:4)

Jesus is the answer to all of your problems and concerns. His Name is above all names. He is King of Kings and Lord of Lords. Nothing is more powerful than Jesus. He's our protector in the midst of a storm.

You know, we only grow spiritually as a result of the storms of life. Storms will come, but Jesus is there in the boat with you. He's been through it all, successfully. Trust Him with your burdens, your hopes and your dreams. Apply the blood of Jesus to yourself, your husband, your wife, your children, your dog and your cat, your home and property, your apartment. Nothing...no nothing....no demon, no problem can ever be successful against the Blood of Jesus. Look to Jesus for even the little problems in life. If you can't trust Jesus with the little things, you won't be able to trust Him when the big storms come. Trust Him, trust Him, trust Him, and the peace of God will always be inside of you.

(Thanks and acknowledgement given for the following article taken off the computer.)

Jesus is GOD. He is the first and last, the beginning and the end! He's the keeper of Creation and the creator of all! He's the architect of the universe and the manager of all times. He always was, always is, and He always will be...unmoved, unchanged, undefeated and never undone! He was bruised and brought healing! He was pierced and eased pain! He was persecuted and brought freedom! He was dead and brought life! He is risen and brings power! He reigns and brings peace! The world can't understand Him, the armies can't defeat Him, the schools can't explain Him and the leaders can't ignore Him. Herod couldn't kill Him. The Pharisees couldn't confuse Him and the people couldn't hold Him. Nero couldn't crush Him. Hitler couldn't silence Him. The New Age can't replace Him and Oprah can't explain Him away. He is light, love, longevity and Lord. He is goodness, kindness, gentleness, and God. He is holy, righteous, mighty, powerful and pure. His ways are right. His word is eternal. His will is unchanging, and His mind is on me. He's my Savior. He's my guide and He's my peace! He's my joy, my comfort and my Lord and He rules my life! I serve Him because His bond is love, His burden is light and His goal for me is abundant life. I follow Him because He is the wisdom of the wise, the power of the powerful, the ancient of days, the ruler or rulers, the leader of leaders, the overseer of the overcomers, and is to come. And if that seems impressive to you, try this for size: His goal is a relationship with ME! He will never leave me, never forsake me, never mislead me, never forget me, never overlook me and never cancel my appointment in His appointment book! When I fall He lifts me up! When I fail He forgives! When I am weak, He is strong! When I am lost, He is the way! When I am afraid He is my courage! When I stumble, He steadies me! When I am hurt, He heals me! When I am broken, He mends me! When I am blind, He leads me! When I am hungry, He feeds me! When I face trials, He is with me! When I face persecution, He shields me! When I face problems, He comforts me! When I face loss, He provides for me! When I face death, He carries me home! He is everything for everybody everywhere, every time and every way. He is God. He is faithful. I am His and He is mine! My Father in heaven can whip the father of this world. God is in control and I am on His side and that means all is well with my soul. He is God!

CHAPTER 3

****

WHO AM I?

****

When Jesus was here on earth He was fully human as well as fully God. He came to suffer and die for each one of us. He was a servant. He came to serve, teach, heal and to die. No one was ever more humiliated than Jesus before He died. He was insulted, spat upon, whipped, beaten, nailed to a cross. But now He's no longer in that role. Now, in Heaven at the right side of God the Father, He is our Savior, Righteous God. On the cross He said it. "It is finished". In 1 John 4:17 the Bible tells us that as Jesus is (present tense) so are we in this world. Jesus said the works that HE did, we will do also, and even greater works we would do. As a Christian we are capable of doing all the things that Jesus did and even more. What did He do? Signs and wonders and miracles! What didn't He do? He didn't sin. Jesus loved and forgave His enemies. Look at who you are! This is exciting. You are fearfully and wonderfully made. You are marvelous darling!!!!

It's true, in the natural, that we're unworthy and sinners saved by grace. It takes no faith to say these things. But God has taken us far beyond that. He sees the finished product. Remember, without faith it's impossible to please God. So by faith we need to see ourselves as God sees us and by faith we need to say what God says we are. The Bible tells us as a man/woman thinks, so is he/she (Proverbs 23:7). What you think about yourself is what comes to be.

God raised Jesus from the dead and seated Him at His right Hand in Heaven...FAR above all rule and authority and power and dominion and every name that is named. He has put all things under His (Jesus') feet and appointed Him the universal Head of the church, which is His body. Ephesians 1:20-23.

Take your rightful place Christian. Did you know that God esteems His children more highly than Himself? What?????? When I first learned this from John Bevere's book Honor's Reward, I was astounded! Well, first I looked up the word esteem. What exactly does esteem mean? The dictionary states it means "to think highly of, to consider or regard, favorable opinion, respect." Philippians 2:3 "Let nothing be done through selfish ambition or conceit, but in lowliness of mind, let each esteem others better than himself." 1 Peter 2:24. Jesus "hung on the cross for our sins, sickness, diseases, poverty and judgment because He esteemed you better than Himself." Romans 12:10 "Be kindly affectionate to one another with brotherly love, in honor giving preference to one another. Jesus is the first born of many brothers and sisters. Romans 8:29. We're commanded to love one another as Jesus has loved us. John 13:34. Jesus <u>died</u> for you! Your Daddy is the King most high. With God all things are possible. Take back what the devil has stolen from you and then destroy his camp!

When you don't know who you are and what rights you have as a believer in Jesus, you will be defeated. On the other hand, when you do know who you are, what rights you have and the power you have in the Name of Jesus, you will be victorious...So, WHO AM I?

I am the salt of the earth.

Matthew 5:13

I am the light of the world.

Matthew 5:14

I am a child of God.   John 1:12

I am part of the true vine, and Christ's life flows through me.   John 15:1, 5

I am Christ's friend.   John 15:15

I am chosen by Christ to bear fruit.

John 15:16

I am Christ's personal witness sent out to tell everyone about Him.   Acts 1:8

I am a slave to righteousness.   Romans 6:18

I am a slave to God, making me holy and giving me eternal life.   Romans 6:22

I am a child of God. I can call Him my Father.
                    Romans 8:14, 15; Galatians 3:26; 4:6

I am a coheir with Christ, inheriting His glory.
                                                    Romans 8:17

I am a temple—a dwelling place for God. His Spirit and His life live in me.
                              1 Corinthians 3:16; 6:19

I am joined to the Lord and am one spirit with Him.   1 Corinthians 6:17

I am a part of Christ's body.
                              1 Corinthians 12:27

I am a new person in Christ. My past is forgiven and everything is new.
                                    2 Corinthians 5:17

I am at peace with God and He has given me the work of helping others to find peace with Him.   2 Corinthians 5:18, 19

I am a child of God and one with others in His family.   Galatians 3:26, 28

I am a child of God and will receive the inheritance He has promised.   Galatians 4:6-7

I am a saint, a holy person.
Ephesians 1:1,Philippians 1:1;
Colossians 1:2

The sinful person I used to be died with Christ and sin no longer rules my life.
Romans 6:1-6

I am free from the punishment (condemnation) my sin deserves.   Romans 8:1

I have been placed into Christ by God's doing.   1 Corinthians 1:30

I have received God's Spirit into my life. I can recognize the blessings He has given me.   1 Corinthians 2:12

I have been given the mind of Christ. He gives me His wisdom to make right choices.
1 Corinthians 2:16

I have been bought with a price. I am not my own. I belong to God. 1 Corinthians 6:19-20

I am God's possession, chosen and secure in Him (sealed). I have been given the Holy Spirit as a promise of my inheritance to come.   Ephesians 1:13-14

Since I have died, I no longer live for myself, but for Christ.   2 Corinthians 5:14-15

I have been made acceptable to God (righteous)   2 Corinthians 5:21

I have been crucified with Christ, and it is no longer I who live, but Christ lives in me. The life I now live is Christ's life.
                                              Galatians 2:20

I have been blessed with every spiritual blessing   Ephesians 1:3

I was chosen in Christ to be holy before the world was created. I am without blame before Him.   Ephesians 1:4

I was chosen by God (predestined) to be adopted as His child.   Ephesians 1:5

I have been brought out of slavery to sin (redeemed) and forgiven. I have received His generous grace.   Ephesians 1:7-8

I am a citizen of heaven with all of God's
family.   Ephesians 2:19

I am God's building Project; His handiwork,
created in Christ to do His work.
                                 Ephesians 2:10

I am a citizen of Heaven, with all of God's
family. I am a prisoner of Christ, so I can help
others.   Ephesians 3:1; 4:1

I am righteous and holy.   Ephesians 4:24

I am hidden with Christ in God.
                                 Colossians 3:3

I am an expression of the life of Christ because
He is my life.   Colossians 3:4

I am chosen of God, holy and dearly loved.
        Colossians 3:12; 1 Thessalonians 1:4

I am a child of light and not of darkness.
                                 1 Thessalonians 5:5

I am chosen to share in God's heavenly
calling   Hebrews 3:1

I am part of Christ. I share in His life.
                                 Hebrews 3:14

I am one of God's living stones, being built up in Christ as a spiritual house. 1 Peter 2:5

I am a member of a chosen race, a royal priesthood, a holy nation, a people belonging to God.   1 Peter 2:9-10

I am only a visitor to this world in which I temporarily live.   1 Peter 2:11

I am an enemy of the devil.   1 Peter 5:8

I am a child of God, and I will be like Christ when He returns.   1 John 3:1-2

I am born again in Christ, and the evil one—the devil—cannot touch me.   1 John 5:18

I am not the great "I Am", but by the grace of God, I am what I am.
                    Exodus 3:14; John 8:28, 18, 58,
                              1 Corinthians 15:10

Since I am in Christ, by the grace of God, I am now acceptable to God, (justified) and completely forgiven. I live at peace with Him.   Romans 5:1, 9; 3:26; 5:9

I have been made spiritually alive, just as Christ is alive.   Ephesians 2:5

I have been raised up and seated with Christ
in heaven.   Ephesians 2:6

I have direct access to God through the
Spirit.   Ephesians 2:18

I may approach God with boldness, freedom,
and confidence.   Ephesians 3:12

I have been rescued from the dark power of
Satan's rule and have been brought into the
kingdom of Christ.   Colossians 1:13

I have been forgiven of all my sins and set free.
The debt against me has been cancelled.
                    Colossians 1:14

Christ Himself lives in me.   Colossians 1:27

I am firmly rooted in Christ and am now being
built up in Him.   Colossians 2:10

I am fully grown (complete) in Christ.
                    Colossians 2:10

I am spiritually clean. My old sinful self has
been removed.   Colossians 2:11

I have been buried, raised and made alive
with Christ.   Colossians 2:12-13

I died with Christ and I have been raised up with Christ. My life is now hidden in Christ, in God. Christ is now my life.

Colossians 3:1-4

I have been given a spirit of power, love, and a sound mind.   2 Timothy 1:7

I have been saved and set apart (sanctified) according to God's plan.

2 Timothy 1:9; Titus 3:5

Because I am set apart (sanctified) and one with Christ, He is not ashamed to call me His brother or sister.   Hebrews 2:11

I have the right to come boldly before the throne of God. He will meet my needs lovingly and kindly.   Hebrews 4:16

In Christ I belong to God.   Ephesians 1:4

Through Christ I am adopted into God's family as His child.   Ephesians 1:5

In Christ I have the mercy and favor of God.

Ephesians 1:6

In Christ I have been forgiven.

Ephesians 1:7

In Christ I have a heavenly inheritance.
Ephesians 1:11

In Christ I received my salvation.
Ephesians 1:13

In Christ the devil is under my feet.
Ephesians 1:22, 23

In Christ I have been granted the mercy and grace of God. Ephesians 2:7-8

In Christ I have been made spiritually new.
Ephesians 2:10

In Christ I have hope and peace.
Ephesians 2:12-14

Through Christ I may come before God.
Ephesians 2:18

Through Christ I am part of the household of God. Ephesians 2:19-22

God's temple and the Holy Spirit permanently live in me. 1 Corinthians 3:16 & 17

I am God's garden; God's building under cultivation. 1 Corinthians 3:9

I belong to Christ and Christ belongs to God. 1 Corinthians 3:23

I must increase and learn in the things of God
and decrease in the things of the flesh.

John 3:30.

HOW TO LOVE YOURSELF
(Thanks to Inspiration daily @ yahoo.com)

Stop all criticism. Criticism never changes a
thing. Refuse to criticize yourself. Accept yourself
exactly as you are. Everybody changes.

When you criticize yourself, your changes
are negative. When you approve of yourself, your
changes are positive.

Don't scare yourself. Stop terrorizing yourself
with your thoughts. It's a dreadful way to live. Find
a mental image that gives you pleasure (i.e. yellow
roses), and immediately switch your scary thought to
a pleasure thought.

Be gentle and kind and patient. Be gentle with
yourself. Be kind to yourself. Be patient with yourself as you learn the new ways of thinking.

Treat yourself as you would someone you really
loved.

Be kind to your mind. Self hatred is hating your
own thoughts. Don't hate yourself for having the
thoughts. Gently change your thoughts.

Praise yourself. Criticism breaks down the inner
spirit. Praise builds it up. Praise yourself as much as
you can. Tell yourself how well you are doing with
every little thing.

Support yourself. Find ways to support yourself.
Reach out to friends and allow them to help you.

It is being strong to ask for help when you need it.

Be loving to your negatives. Acknowledge that you created them to fulfill a need. Now, you are finding new, positive ways to fulfill those needs. So, lovingly release the old negative patterns.

Take care of your body. Learn about nutrition. What kind of fuel does your body need to have optimum energy and vitality? Learn about exercise. What kind of exercise can you enjoy? Cherish and revere the temple you live in.

Mirror work. Look into your eyes often. Express this growing sense of love you have for yourself. Forgive yourself looking into the mirror. Talk to your parents looking into the mirror. Forgive them too. At least once a day say: "I love you, I really love you".

Love yourself. Do it now. Don't wait until you get well, or lose the weight or get the new job, or the new relationship. Begin now—and do the best you can.

Louise L Hay Educational Institute
If you put a small value upon yourself, rest assured that the world will not raise your price.

A DAILY CONFESSION FOR THE NEW YEAR
– by Charles Capps

Father, because of your Word, I have the Spirit of wisdom and knowledge of God. So I covenant

with You now to always give voice to Your Word.
I will never give voice to the words of the enemy.
I will give no place to the devil. But I give place to
the Spirit of God. You have given the angels charge
over me in all my ways, and my way is the way of
the Word. These things will surely come to pass, for
Your Word is within me. I'm redeemed from the cure
of the law. I'm delivered from the powers of darkness. I'm translated into the kingdom of the Son of
God. The Greater One dwells in me, so I'll not fail,
for Your Word is within me.

Your Word will cause me to prevail. Even though
a thousand may fall by my side and ten thousand at
my right hand, it shall not come near me, for You've
given your angels charge over me. They keep me in
all Your ways and in my pathway is life. My pathway
is health. My pathway is prosperity, for Abraham's
blessings are mine!

Christ redeemed me from poverty. He redeemed
me from sickness. He redeemed me from spiritual
death. Therefore, in the Name of Jesus, I give voice
to Your Word. I am the redeemed of the Lord, and
I'm saying so!

I forbid any sickness or disease to operate in my
body. I forbid any tumor or growth to exist in my
body. It disappears. It dissolves. Body, I'm speaking
to you! You come into line with the Word of God!
I'm delivered from growths and tumors. They have
no right to exist. That which God has not planted is
rooted out!

Galatians 3:13 is in my mouth. Galatians 3:13
is flowing in my bloodstream. Galatians 3:13 flows

go every cell of my body. Galatians 3:13 is forming itself in my body. The Word is becoming flesh, for You sent Your Word and healed me.

So Your Word is now being formed in my body. It causes growths to disappear. It causes sickness to flee. It causes arthritis to disappear. My bones and joints function properly. Arthritis, you MUST GO! Sickness, you MUST FLEE! For the Spirit of God is upon me. The Word of God is within me. I will fear no evil, for the Word of the Lord comforts me.

Thus says the Lord: I'm far from oppression. Thus says the Lord: Fear does not come nigh me. Thus says the Lord: No weapon formed against me will prosper, but whatever I do WILL PROSPER! I am the redeemed of the Lord. This is the heritage of the servants of the Lord, and my righteousness is of God!

Heavenly Father, I make a covenant with You to voice Your Word. The Spirit of Truth within me will guide me into all truths. He will teach me all things. He will take of Yours and show it to me. I see these things belong to me. I proclaim now that they are mine! The devil shall not steal them.

I walk in prosperity. I will walk in health, for the Word of God is come unto me. The Greater One is in me. The Greater One will put me over. I will NOT FAIL! I will not fear! I will not tremble when tragedy seems near, for Your Word will destroy the enemy's work and will keep him far from my house.

Even though many may fall by my side, I will proclaim Your Word. Evil will not come near me. I loose the angels. I charge the angels with Your words and the ministering spirits of God to garrison about my home, my family, my finances, and guide me into the wisdom of God. This shall be by the words of my mouth, by the Spirit of God, by the Word of God, and by the angels of God.

Father, You keep me in perfect peace, for my mind is stayed on You. Because of that, I'll not enter the fight, but I'll lift up my hands and rejoice! I'll stand to the true height of Your Word, and I'll not let it go out of my sight. And I will NOT ENTER into the fight! For You will fight for me! The angels of God will work for me, and the Spirit of God within me shall reveal the hidden things.

I confess now that I have perfect knowledge of every situation. I do not lack for the wisdom of God, for I have the mind of Christ. The wisdom of God is formed within me, so I rejoice! The enemy is defeated! God is exalted, and Your Word is Lord of my life!

Father, I covenant with You to be what You said I am. Even though I don't look like it, I may not act like it; I may not feel like it, You said I was, so I must be!

I have overcome! I have overcome the enemy because the Greater One is in me! My faith is the victory that overcomes the world, and it comes by Your Word. So I rejoice! I won't weep in despair. I won't wring my hands and weep in prayer. But I'll come boldly to the Throne of Grace with rejoicing my petition to bear. I'll enter into the new way, and I'll speak the things that You way. And I'll walk in victory, and I'll praise Your Name, and from this day I'll never be the same, in Jesus' Name!

CHAPTER 4

****

IS THERE
REALLY A DEVIL?

****

There has always been God. He never had a beginning. He never will have an ending. There has not always been a devil. Evil did not exist in the beginning. An angel, once known as Lucifer, made himself become a devil, who we know now as Satan. The average Christian believes in God, believes in Jesus, but may not be sure there really is a devil. Bill Johnson, in his book When Heaven Invades Earth states: "At some point we must believe in a God who is big enough to keep us safe in our quest for more of Him. Practically speaking, many Christian's devil is bigger than their God. How can a created, fallen being ever be compared with the infinite Lord of glory? It's an issue of trust. If I focus on my need to protect myself from deception, I will always be over-whelmingly aware of the power of the devil. If my heart is completely turned to the One who is "able to keep me from falling" Jude 24 and, He is the only One I become impressed with. My life reflects what I see with my heart."

We need to be aware that there <u>not only</u> is a devil, but we need to be aware of his activities, what he can and cannot do. Paul tells us in 2 Corinthians 2:10–11, to have forgiveness in order to keep satan from getting the advantage over us, that we are not igno-rant or his wiles and intentions.

Once Lucifer was the most honored angel made by God. He lived in the heavens. His job was to stay at the very throne of God. Lucifer was the smartest, most beautiful angel God ever created. Lucifer was created with a wonderful musical ability. (Ezekiel 28:12-17 "You are the full measure and pattern of exactness (giving the finishing touch to all that constitutes completeness), full of wisdom and perfect in beauty. You were in Eden, the garden of God. Every precious stone was your covering. On the day that you were created they were prepared. You were the anointed cherub that covers with over-shadowing (wings), and I set you so. You were upon the holy mountain of God; you walked up and down in the midst of the stones of fire. You were blameless in your ways from the day you were created until iniquity and guilt were found in you. Through the abundance of your commerce you were filled with lawlessness and violence, and you sinned, therefore; I cast you out as a profane thing from the mountain of God and the guardian Cherub drove you out from the midst of the stones of fire. Your heart was proud and lifted up because of your beauty; you corrupted your wisdom for the sake of your splendor. I cast you to the ground."

Lucifer was created with the ability to make choices. He had been given a free will. He doesn't know everything, like God. If he did know everything then he would have known that Jesus would rise from the dead. 1 Corinthians 2:8.

Lucifer became very proud of himself. He became too proud of himself (1 Timothy 3:6, speaking about the qualifications for someone to hold the office of Bishop in a church congregation): "He must not be a new convert, or he may develop a beclouded and stupid state of mind as the result of pride (be blinded by conceit and fall into the condemnation that the devil once did)."

Lucifer decided in his heart that he would be better than God. In his heart he said: Isaiah 14:13-14 "I will ascent to heaven; I will exalt my throne above the stars of God; I will sit upon the mount of assembly in the uttermost North. I will ascend above the heights of the clouds; I will make myself like the Most High."

This once wonderful angel dared to set himself up to become Almighty God. What a horrible thing for him to even think to plan! He owed God everything because it was God who created him. Many other angels chose to join Lucifer in his plan to rebel against God. It must have been terrible, when God threw Lucifer and his evil followers down from heaven. 2 Peter 2:4 "For God did not even spare angels that sinned, but cast them into hell, delivering them to be kept there in pits of gloom till the judgment and their doom." Luke 10:18 ... Jesus said "I saw satan falling like a lightning flash from the heaven." (to earth...Isaiah 14:12).

And so, Lucifer became known as satan. satan is also called the "god of this world (2 Corinthians 4:4, 1 John 5:19), and was named by Jesus "the prince of this world" (John 14:30). It is possible that a human race created about the same time as Lucifer, who were under Lucifer's rule on earth, probably were convinced to join him in his rebellion against God, and they were destroyed also. Isaiah 14:12 & 16, Ezekiel 28:11-17; Genesis 1:28 "And God blessed them and said to them, be fruitful, multiply and replenish the earth." The bodies of satan and this race of human-like creatures were destroyed and their spirits condemned to be without physical bodies.

It could be that these humans, without bodies, are the "demons" mentioned in the Bible.

satan is present many many places at one time, but only God is present everywhere at one time.

The sin of Lucifer was pride. In my opinion, his sin was the first, original sin in the world.

satan is the accuser of the believers before God. Revelation 12:10; Job 1:8-12; Luke 22:31 & 32; 1 Corinthians 5:5; 1 Timothy 1:20, Zechariah 3:1.

satan has some powers, but only what God permits him to have. Luke 10:19-20, Jesus said that WE have authority and power over all the power that the devil and demons possess, and NOTHING shall in any way harm the believer.

Revelation 20:10 AND Isaiah 14:15 state that the devil will be cast into the Lake of Fire "Then the devil who had lead them them astray deceiving and seducing them, was hurled into the fiery lake of burning brimstone where the beast and false prophet were, and they will be tormented day and night forever and ever. (through the ages of the ages)."

And, after all these thousands of years, he still doesn't get it. He's lost!!! He's under our feet. Christ is our Head. Believers are Christ's Body. All things are under Jesus' feet. We're His Body. We're Jesus' hands. We're Jesus' feet, so, the devil is under OUR FEET! We can defeat satan not by the Blood of the Lamb, Jesus Christ and speaking the Word of God. Revelation 12:11. "The devil was a murderer from the beginning, and abode not in the truth, because there is no truth in him. When he speaks a lie, he speaks of his own, for he is a liar and the father of it." John 8:44 satan is a liar. He looks to deceive us and to distort our thinking. He works at it through our mind. Therefore, we need to cleanse our minds of any negative, wrong thinking 2 Corinthians 10:3-5). If he can control our mind, he can control our behavior. All behavior begins first in the mind before it becomes actual acted on behavior. We need to resist satan and he will flee from us. James 4:7. The Bible tells us "as a man (or woman) thinks, so he (she) is. Proverbs 23:7.

satan is evil in perfection. He is always looking to destroy God's creation. From the beginning of time he's been "the father of lies" John 8:44 and a deceiver 2 Thessalonians 2:10. He continues to wrongfully accuse God and His people Revelation 12:10, Zechariah 3:1. He even misled the fallen unholy angels that joined with him in his revolution against God. Daniel 8:10 & 12, Revelation 12:4.

satan's oldest trick is self deception. Genesis 3. He deceived Eve back in the Garden of Eden in her desire, like his, to be like God. He deceived her into thinking he was there for HER, that he was being nice to her for her gain. Instead he was looking to deceive her in order to hurt God, through the rebellion of the child. It's no different today. satan is looking to destroy the world, you and me, and keep people from God. John 10:10. God created the world and His people for good. We were meant to enjoy God, to enjoy life and the world we were placed in. satan knows he's doomed to hell and he wants to take as many with him as he possibly can. John 16:7-11, Revelation 2:12.

Jesus said the devil is a thief that comes to steal, kill and destroy. But Jesus came that we might have life and more abundantly. That means here in the some times "nasty now and now" and then later on too, in the "sweet by and by. John 10:10.

satan must be resisted. James 4:7. Jesus robbed him of his rights to accuse us. Romans 8:33-34, to kill us. Colossians 1:13 and to own us. Colossians 1:13 and 2:15. (Thanks to Pastor David Garcia for these points). If we surround ourselves with and give ourselves over to satanic power we will destroy our lives here on earth and end up in hell in eternity. On the other hand, if we surround ourselves with and give ourselves over to God's power, then we will live fruitful lives here on earth and our eternal destination is heaven. It's that simple. 1 John 5:12 "He who has the Son has life; he who does not have the Son of God does not have life."

The opposite of life is death.

NAMES/REFERENCES TO satan

satan
SATANAS
AN ADVERSARY
AN OPPONENT IN BATTLE - 1 Samuel 29:4
POLITICAL ADVERSARY – 1 Kings 11:14
THE DEVIL, DIABOLOS (THE SLANDERER)
Matthew 4:1; Luke 4:2; John 8:44; Ephesians 6:11;
     Revelation 12:12
ABADDON or APOLLYON - Revelation 9:11
ACCUSER   OF   OUR   BROTHERS-Revelation
     12:10
ENEMY – 1 Peter 5:8
BEELZEBUB – Matthew 12:24
BELIAL – 2 Corinthians 6:15
THE ONE WHO LEADS THE WHOLE WORLD
     ASTRAY Revelation 12:9
THE EVIL ONE – Matthew 13:19, 38;
1 John 2:13, 5:19
A MURDERER – John 8:44
THE FATHER OF LIES – John 8:44
THE god OF THIS AGE – 2 Corinthians 4:4
THAT ANCIENT SERPENT – Revelation 12:9

THE PRINCE OF THIS WORLD – John 12:31;
John 14:30
THE RULER OF THE KINGDOM OF THE AIR
– Ephesians 2:2
THE TEMPTER – Matthew 4:5; 1 Thessalonians
3:5

These titles of satan were taken from the NIV
Compact Dictionary of the Bible, 1989

CHECK YOURSELF OUT FOR satan's INFLUENCE

LUST: Improper sexual thoughts, unclean actions;
using others for your own pleasure.

IDOLS: Anything that comes between you and God,
i.e. family, job, vacations, daily business, hobby,
exercise, your diet.

LAZY: Tired, overworked, commitments as reasons
for not being involved in the things of God.

TOUCHY: Does everyone have to agree with you?
Are you often and easily offended? Always
trying to prove yourself? Have to be in charge of
everything?

JUDGING: Are you measuring others by yourself? They should do this....they should do that.
Disapproval of people's looks, dress, car, how
well they clean their house, vacations, running

their church, using their time, spending or saving their money, raising their children. Do you have a better ministry than they do?

UNCOMPROMISING: Do you disagree and then leave the church?

CONTROLLING? Do you seek to compromise? Are you flexible or do you have your own agenda? Do you have to have your own way? Are you submissive to your husband, to your Pastor? It's MY way or the highway!!!! Got a chip in your shoulder?

GOSSIP: Do you enjoy passing on a bad report? Did you hear such and such? Just so we can pray about it…"

WORRYING: What to you worry about? When you worry you're telling God that He's not big enough, not powerful enough to take care of it.

NEGATIVITY: Is the glass half full or half empty? Do you have ANYTHING good to say? Always see the dark side of things. Self pity, poor me. Always looking for a fight. Using your negative past as an excuse for your present behavior?

DOUBTFUL: Do you wonder if your salvation is real? If things written in the Bible are real? If God is able to heal? Doubt is a sin.

SELFISH: Do you ignore the needs of others and put your own desires first? Don't tithe. Give only as little as you think you can get away with?

EASILY DISTRACTED: Easily distracted. Do you find it hard to sit down and read the Bible? Pray? Do you keep getting up to do other things? Do you finish tasks you start or do you go from one thing to another to another, finishing nothing?

LYING: Saying things that aren't true to make the story sound better? Or to cover yourself? A lie is a lie!

DISSATISFIED: All the time, with your job, your husband or wife or children, your home, your church. They don't do this or that. I don't need anyone or anything. Everyone else has the problem, not me. They didn't do it that way in my other church?

DISCOURAGED: All the time if things don't work out at the first try. You just stop trying and quit. Fear or success, fear of failure. Is it too tough to work out things in your marriage, easier to get a divorce?

WASTE TIME: We need time for God, time for family. Do you spend most of your off time watching TV?

ABUSIVE: Do you always just speak out what's on your mind, even if it hurts others? Do you have a bad temper? Are your kids, wife, husband afraid of you?

ENVY: Do you have to keep up with the Jones? Do you get angry when someone is blessed? Or are you happy for them?

DEPRESSION: Always thinking about your problems or someone else's. Are you in a sad mood all the time? Is life too much for you to handle? Are you lonely? Do you have low self esteem? Feel interior? Thought about suicide? Planned it?

FEAR: Are you afraid of life, death, heights, the dark, people, sickness, poverty, war, anthrax, end times, afraid to witness for Jesus? Are you always anxious about things?

PROCRASTINATION: Are you always busy and never getting anything done? Are you organized? "I'll do it later. Tomorrow is another day." Later, later, it's always later.

DISRESPECTFUL: Do you speak negatively about your spouse, children, Pastor, relatives, neighbors...people in general? Do you see only their faults? Do you have difficulty trusting people? Are you jealous with your husband/wife?

<u>ARE YOU A LONER?</u> Have you been hurt by family, friends, church people? "I don't need to belong to a church. I can just visit different churches...or I can just stay home and watch so and so on TV."

<u>PRIDE</u>: "I did this. I did that. I did it all by myself. Nobody helped me. I ready my Bible more than anyone else I know. I pray 3 hours a day. My husband's just not on the spiritual level that I'm on."

These outward symptoms are expressions of something that's going on inside.

God has only good plans for you.
Jeremiah 29:11

CHAPTER 5

****

WHAT CAUSES SICKNESS?

****

In Genesis 2:15-17, we have God's instructions:

> "And the Lord God took the man and put him in the Garden of Eden to tend and guard and keep it. And the Lord God commanded the man, saying: You may freely eat of every tree of the garden, but of the Tree of the Knowledge of Good and Evil and Blessing and Calamity you shall not eat, for in the day that you eat of it, you shall surely die."

In chapter 3 of Genesis, we have the account of Adam and Eve's disobedience and punishment and the ground was cursed.

In Deuteronomy, God gave us His laws. In Deuteronomy 28:1-14, God lists potential blessings. In Deuteronomy 28:15-68, God lists potential curses imposed for disobedience.

Sickness can be caused by disobedience (sin). Deuteronomy 28:15-68.

Sickness can be caused by improper or incomplete Nutrition:

a) FOOD – Romans 14:20 tells us "You must NOT for the sake of food, destroy the work of God." The work of God is US. Mike Murdock has said "Christian people have faith to believe for healing, but not for health. They will not spend any time on striving for divine health – i.e. no exercise, poor eating habits."

God's original plan for man was for him to be a vegetarian. In Genesis 1:29 we read that man was given every herb and every tree for food.

This was true for the animal world as well. People who lived in this time frame lived over 900 years. After the flood, people lived to be only a little over 100 years of age. After the flood, meat was introduced for man to eat and the fear of man was put into the animal. Genesis 9:1-4. Every moving thing became a potential meal for mankind. Of course the animals alive then did not consume any chemicals and hormones like our food today. With the Law later being introduced to man, God gave instructions as to which animals were acceptable for consumption, some being "clean" while others were declared "unclean". Dietary laws are found in Deuteronomy 4 and Leviticus 11.

What did Jesus eat?

1) fruits and vegetables, whole grain bread
2) only clean meat, poultry and fish. Fish was probably his main "meat".

Jesus said in Luke 5:31: "It is not those who are healthy who need a physician, but those who are sick." If you have a sickness, it's perfectly good for you to go to a physician. God gave mankind knowledge. GOD is the healer, not your physician.

b) WATER
c) CHEMICALS IN FOOD

Sickness can be caused by improper behavior:

a) Lack of exercise
b) Smoking
c) Unnatural sexual behavior
d) Alcohol
e) Drug use, prescription and illegal
f) Participating in occult activities

Sickness can come because we do not tithe. Malachi 3:10. Sickness can be caused by an attack from satan, i.e. The woman bowed over. Luke 13:10-16.

It can be caused by speaking against a man or woman of God. i.e. Miriam and Aaron speaking against Moses. Numbers 12:1-9.

Sickness can be caused by generational curses. Exodus 20:4 & 5. It can be caused by ethnic traditions.

Sickness can be caused by receiving the Lord's Supper (communion) unworthily....with sin, with bad attitude. 1 Corinthians 11:27. Wrong attitudes and behavior can cause premature death. We need to get our life right with God. Are you in the habit of cursing, using God's Name?

Sickness can be caused by unforgiveness and bitterness towards people.

It can be caused by opening spiritual doors to demonic spirits. There are many kinds of spirits:

SPIRIT OF JEALOUSY

Impatience, bitterness, strife, covetousness, control (Jezebel), revenge/retaliation/wrath, suspicion, anger/rage, murder/violence, restlessness/selfishness. Numbers 5:14, 30

FAMILIAR SPIRITS

Spirit guides, inherited curses, curses from: occult/roots/voodoo, words that have been spoken 1 Samuel 28:3, 8-9, Deuteronomy 18:11; 2 Kings 23:24; Isaiah 8:19

SPIRIT OF WHOREDOM / PERVERSION

Prostitution, cults/religious, legalism/tradition, idolatry, emotional weakness, fornication/adultery, word twisting, lust, lesbianism/homosexuality, masturbation, sodomy/bestiality, child molestation, incest, exhibitionism/pornography, seducing spirit, sensual thoughts. Zechariah 13:2, Hosea 4:12, 5:2

SPIRITS OF RELIGIOUS CONTROL

(Jezebel), Daniel 10:13 & 20

SPIRIT OF HEAVINESS

Gloominess/sadness, rejection/despair, grief/fatigue, guilt, self-pity/loneliness, depression, manic depression, suicide/insomnia. 1 Samuel 1:10, Isaiah 61:3, Luke 8:26-39

HAUGHTY SPIRITS

Pride/perfection, accusation, competition, mockery, stubbornness, self-righteousness, gossip/boastful, sarcastic/critical. Proverbs 16:18; 1 Samuel 13:8-14; 1 Samuel 14-23

UNCLEAN, IMPURE OR FOUL SPIRITS

Mark 7:25

SEXUALLY SEDUCTIVE SPIRITS

Genesis 6:4

SPIRITS OF ANTI-CHRIST

Doubt and unbelief, rebellion, witchcraft, self exaltation. 1 John 4:1-3

EVIL SPIRITS

Luke 7:21; Luke 8:2, Acts 19:12

LYING SPIRIT

Deception/lies, exaggeration, profanity, hypoc-risy, condemning others, theft/isolation, vanity. 1 Timothy 4:1, 1 John 4:6, 1 Kings 22:21-23

SPIRIT OF DIVINATION

Occult/magic (black or white). Acts 16:16

SPIRIT OF FEAR

Insecurity/inadequacy, inferiority complex, timidity/worry, Sensitivity/fear of authority, terror/torment/horror, nightmares/panic attacks, phobias, anxiety/nervousness, abandonment, procrastination. Romans 8:15, 1 John 4:6, 1 Timothy 4:1

SPIRIT OF INFIRMITY

Inherited curses (infirmities), arthritis, asthma/ hay fever/allergies, fever/cancer, early death, every disease/pain. Matthew 8:16 17, Mark 9:22, 1 Samuel 16:14, also known as::

a)	sickness	Luke 5:15
b)	diseases	Luke 8:2
c)	crippling spirit	Luke 13:11

SPIRIT OF INVALID

John 5:5

DEAF AND DUMB SPIRIT

Mental illness, insanity, seizures, epilepsy, double mindedness, multi-personality (nicknames), hyperactivity, self-mutilation. Matthew 9:32 & 33, Mark 9:25

SPIRIT OF TREACHERY

Judges 9:23

SPIRIT OF SLUMBER OR DEEP SLEEP (SPIRITUAL DULLNESS OR BLINDNESS)

Withdrawal, mind binding, sleepiness, forgetful-ness, stupidity, daydreaming, trances, laziness, lethargy, sluggishness/confusion. Isaiah 29:10; Romans 11:8, Isaiah 19:14

Thanks to New Beginnings Christian Counseling Center for their resources.
Why is there sickness?

Because of sin, we are afflicted. But God sent Jesus and He healed us.   Psalm 107:17-20.

Because we live in a cursed world.
                                                              Genesis 3:17.

The Blood of Jesus brings healing and deliverance as well as salvation.

IS HEALING SCRIPTURAL?
WHY ARE SOME NOT HEALED?
HOW DOES GOD HEAL?
****

Healing is God's will for us. Jesus, the Great Physician, said that those who believe shall lay hands on the sick and they shall recover. Mark 16:18. Is it REALLY God's will for people to be healed? Let's see what the Word of God says.

Matthew 3:1-3 The leper said to Jesus – "If you want to, you can heal me." And Jesus' reply was – "I want to, be healed." In Hebrews 13:8, we're told that Jesus Christ is "the same, yesterday, today and forever."

Jesus said in John 14:12 "I assure you, most solemnly, I tell you, if anyone steadfastly believes in Me, he will himself be able to do the things that I do, and he will do even greater things than these because I go to the Father."

Acts 10:38 says: "How God anointed and consecrated Jesus of Nazareth with the Holy Spirit and with strength and ability and power and how He went about doing good and in particular, curing all who were harassed and oppressed by the power of the devil, for God was with Him." Sickness and disease are from the devil.

1 John 3:8 "The reason the Son of God was made manifest (visible) was to undo (destroy, loosen and dissolve) the works the devil (has done)."

What are the conditions of healing?

We must have awe, a fear, and a reverence of God. Proverbs 3:5 "Lean on, trust and be confident in the Lord with all your heart and mind, and do not rely on your own insight or understanding."

We must trust and rely on God, seven days a week, not just for an hour on Sunday.

Proverbs 3:6-8 "In all your ways know, recognize and acknowledge Him (God) and He will direct and make straight and plain your paths. Be not wise in your own eyes – reverently fear and worship the Lord and turn entirely away from evil"...verse 8 says "It shall be health to your nerves and sinews and marrow and moistening to your bones."

We must turn completely away from evil. We must make up our minds to live sinless lives each day. You can't live like a saint on Sunday and "like hell" the rest of the week. God's not a fool. He will not be mocked.

When we think of sin, we usually think of the "big" sins. But there are lots of others that are equally sin that many of us do on a daily basis, and never think of it as:

S I N

LUST
PORNOGRAPHY
LYING
CHEATING ON INCOME TAX
GOSSIP
BACK-BITING/COMPLAINING
DISRESPECTING OTHERS
WORRY
PESSIMISM/NEGATIVITY
LAZINESS/DISTRACTION/
PROCRASTINATION
TOUCHINESS/SELFISHNESS
JUDGMENTAL
IDOLATRY (ANYTHING THAT GETS FIRST
    PLACE BEFORE GOD.)
DOUBT
SELFISHNESS
DISTRACTION
UNFORGIVENESS

This is surely and realistically only a partial list of examples of sin.

Does God heal the "heathen" (unsaved) person? Yes, sometimes He does. We have to remember always, that <u>GOD IS SOVEREIGN.</u>

God expects us to take care of our body: Proper nutrition, food, water, rest, exercise. Whether you agree with me or not,

SMOKING
OVEREATING
ALCOHOL
ILLEGAL DRUGS
POOR EATING HABITS, OBESITY, BEING A
COUCH POTATO, MOST FAST FOODS, DIET
DRINKS

Are NOT GOOD for your body. We need to learn to take proper care of our body.

Hebrews 11:6: "But without faith it is impossible to please Him—for he that comes to God must believe that He is and that He is a Rewarder of them that diligently seek Him." We have to believe that God exists and that He rewards those who seek Him.

God wants us to seek after Him, to seek His face and not His Hand. We need to daily read His Word.

We find time to read newspapers and magazines, the TV listings, and watch endless hours of television. Put time with God first on your list of priorities. We need to learn to listen for God. When you listen to God, you need to be quiet. Get rid of all outside distractions. We need to be doers of the Word of God, not just hearers of the Word. Special meetings with special speakers, prophets and teachers are great, but we also need to put into practice, to do those things we're being taught to do.

Why are some not healed?

No one really has the answer to this question. We must always remember that God is sovereign. All healing comes from God, whether it's supernatural, through physicians and hospital staff, or in death. GOD is the Healer. God can and will do anything He wants to do. He does things His way. "He (God) does as He pleases with the powers of heaven and the peoples of the earth. No one can hold back His hand or say to Him "What have you done?" Daniel 4:34. The bottom line here is that we have to do things God's way, not ours. God is Sovereign. GOD IS GOD. He knows the beginning from the end.

Sometimes He works circumstances together for His desired end result. God has a plan for our lives. He knows the future. Isaiah 55:7-11. We can look to Romans 8:28 "And we know that all things work together for good to them that love God, to them who are called according to His purpose. Everything works out in agreement with the counsel and design of God's Will. Ephesians 1:11. I remember an illustration I read on this very thing: Imagine that you are God, and you're up in the high eternity. You're looking down at earth and seeing all that is happening. You see that there will be an accident ahead and so, you try to warn your child. But your child is busy doing what they want to do, even good stuff. You try to warn them, but they won't listen…and so the accident happens. I find, in my life, that the times when I have had the greatest "thrust" of spiritual growth have been in trying, upsetting times. In times of crisis, I think we all turn our attention more on God, to get us out of the situation, at least. Maybe we even promise Him that we won't stray from Him again, only to stray again after the crisis is over. Sometimes, I think, God allows things to come at us, to GET our attention.

God wants us to love Him. We need to seek Him, spend time with Him like we do with those whom we love. If you truly love someone, you never want to deliberately hurt them. You want to constantly be with them. Remember talking on the phone for hours with your boyfriend or girlfriend, even though you had just left them after being physically WITH THEM for hours before. You just couldn't get enough of them. All you talked about was them! Some people think about God as a "blessing machine" and only want what WE want, what comes out of His Hand.

If you make your faith confessions and do all soul-searching and healing does not seem to come, seek medical help, without condemnation.

Some are not healed due to a lack of faith for healing. Faith is believing in what you have not actually seen. Hebrews 11:1

The book of James tells us that "faith without works is dead". James 2:20

3 John 1:2 tells us that it is God's Will for us to prosper and be in health, even as our soul prospers.

We need to pray God's Will...and His Will is His Word. Luke 22:42. We must ACT in faith. Put action to your belief. Do something you couldn't do before, even if it hurts. Healing is not usually instantaneous, though it can be. Miracles are instant. Healing can come so gradually you may not even realize it is happening till it's all gone!

James 5:15 & 16 tells us to confess our sins to one another—to pray for one another that you may be healed. Sometimes, praying for others brings about our own healing.

Malachi 4:2 says "For you who fear My Name, the Sun of Righteousness will rise with healing in His Wings. A condition for healing here is for us to fear God, esteem God, and respect God.

Why are some not healed? That's a tough question. I don't think we'll ever be able to answer that one really. Bad things happen to good people.

God tells us in His Word that He will have mercy and compassion upon whomever HE desires. Healing is dependent upon God's mercy. We are reminded in 1 Corinthians 1:25 that God is wiser and stronger than man. In Romans 11:34-36 and 1 Corinthians 2:11-16 the Bible asks us "Who can know the thoughts of God?" And the answer, of course, is "No one, except God reveals His thoughts to man." Who are we to question God? Isaiah 29:16 and 45:9. We were created by God for HIS purposes. We've not created anything. Our Pastor, David Garcia puts it well. He says: "You can ask God questions, but don't question God."

Although we wonder why these things happen, we can't question God's purpose. We're really only left to trust that He knows best. God is telling us that everything will be fine in the end.

Do bad things happen to people because they are bad or because they deserve it? In Luke 13:1-5, 11-16. Jesus replied to people who brought Him bad news that people had died. Were the people who died greater sinners than other people, they asked Him. Twice He told them "No." But He also warned them to prepare for eternity or they would be eternally lost. Evil spirits and generational curses can cause infirmity. God is patient and long suffering waiting for us to come to Him. He wants us to repent, to turn from our sinful ways. He's waiting for us to realize that we're sinners and we need to be forgiven. It's the only way to Heaven for any of us.

In Psalm 68:20 the Bible tells us "to God alone belong the escapes from death."

Hebrews 2:8 tells us that everything was put under the subjection of man, but presently, even back then in Jesus' day man was not completely in control of things. Man did have control of everything in the Garden of Eden but he disobeyed God and lost that dominion. Earth came under satan's control as a result of mankind's fall, and with that came physical and spiritual death.

Bill Johnson in his book When Heaven Invades Earth puts it well. He says "God does as He pleases. While true to His Word, He does not avoid acting outside of our understanding of it. For example, He's a loving God who hates Esau (Malachi 1:2 & 3). He's the One who has been respectfully called a gentleman, yet who knocked Saul off of his donkey (Acts 9:4). and picked Ezekiel up off the ground by his hair (Ezekiel 8:3). He's the bright and Morning star (Revelation 22:16) who veils Himself in darkness (Psalm 97:2). He hates divorce yet is Himself divorced (Jeremiah 3:8). This list of seemingly conflicting ideas could go on for much longer than any of us could bear. Yet this uncomfortable tension is designed to keep us honest and truly dependent on the Holy Spirit for understanding who God is and what He is saying to us through His book. God is so foreign to our natural ways of thinking that we only truly see what He shows us—and we can only understand Him through relationship. The Bible is the absolute Word of God. It reveals God; the obvious, the unexplainable, the mysterious, and sometimes offensive. It all reveals the greatness of our God. Yet it does not contain Him. God is bigger than His book."

Why does God let bad things happen to good people? (Thanks to Patrick Conaty for these resources.)

We see how devastating evil can be. It is a reminder to seek what is good and to seek God.

It helps develop character. It helps us to endure, and endurance builds character. Character enables us to handle tough situations and to help others who are going through similar suffering.

To get our attention. Sometimes when we're doing wrong things Jesus uses suffering to get our attention. It can bring us closer to Him or make us angry and we pull away from Him.

How does God heal?

God heals through many different methods. Healing is either instant...this is a miracle, or gradual.

Of course we all want that miracle, but many times our healing comes so gradually that it takes us a while to realize that it has happened.

When someone has prayed for you and in the natural you do not see or feel anything different in the condition, do not despair and feel that God has not done anything. Instead keep silent in this regard. Speak no negative. "Well, I guess that God didn't heal me". Speak only positive and expect it to happen. "I believe I'm healed. Thank you Lord for my healing", even when you don't see it yet. Some of the methods God uses in healing are:

Laying hands on the sick. Mark 16:17 & 18 "And these signs shall follow them that believe; in My Name shall they cast out devils, they shall speak with new tongues; they shall lay hands on the sick and they shall recover.

You have to believe that healing is still for today. If you don't believe healing is for today, the sick won't recover when you lay hands on them, nor will YOU be healed. If you don't believe its true, it WON'T happen. You CAN lay hands on yourself and pray for yourself.

By going under the power of the Holy Spirit.
By the gift of faith in the one doing the praying.
By the gift of faith in the one being prayed for.
By command in Jesus' Name.
By the person being prayed for putting their faith into action.

Luke 6:19 Everyone was trying to touch Jesus. When they did, they were cured.

Mark 6:56 "They would lay the sick in the marketplaces and beg Him that they might touch even the fringe of His outer garment, and as many as touched Him were restored to health."

Acts 1:8 "But you shall receive power (ability, efficiency, and might) when the Holy Spirit has come upon you." Example MARK 5:25-34 The woman with the issue of blood.

Talk to the mountain! Mark 11:23 "Truly I tell you, whoever says to this mountain, be lifted up and thrown into the sea! And does not doubt at all in his heart but believes that what he says will take place, it will be done for him." When you pray petition prayer, you are asking God for something. When you COMMAND IN Jesus' Name, you are ORDERING something. In Mark 11:23, it tells us to talk to the mountain, not to God. We need to confess (believe) by saying with OUR MOUTH, whatever we expect to see happen. You have to EXPECT that it WILL HAPPEN. Our confession that we are healed is necessary until the manifestation comes. "I believe I've received my healing." "Thank you Jesus, by Your Stripes, I AM healed." You have to be able to "see" yourself healed. "See" yourself doing an activity that you've been unable to do. – GOD IS NOT A RESPECTER OF PERSONS.

Isaiah 53:5 & 10: By Jesus' stripes, we ARE healed and made whole.

When Jesus was on that cross, He took all diseases and illnesses upon Himself. He was beaten with 39 lashes. There are 39 major diseases. Jesus took all of them upon Himself.

Anointing with oil.
James 5:14 & 15; Mark 6:12 & 13

Intercessory prayer. Matthew 8, The Centurion said "Speak the word only and my servant shall be healed." People stand in for others, asking for prayer for someone not physically present. There is no distance with God.

Healing can occur through the use of prayer cloths. ACTS 19:11 & 12 There is power in a piece of cloth when the anointing of God rests on it.

Healing can occur through faith in action. MATTHEW 12:10 & 13 – A withered hand.

Give someone a task to do that they were previously unable to perform. The same incident is recorded in Mark 3:1-5 and Luke 6:6-10, John 9: 6 & 7 – A blind man...Jesus made clay with His spit and placed the clay on the blind man's eyes and told him to go wash it off. The healing occurred when the blind man put his faith into action.

I experienced this some years ago. A sudden physical attack came against me. I awoke suddenly, in the middle of the night, had nausea and sweats that poured off me like someone had placed me under a shower, and this was followed by extreme weakness. After this, all I wanted to do was sleep. My husband-to-be, Fred, stayed with me and prayed for me. The weakness and sleep continued. The next day was Sunday and I was a Sunday school teacher. "How am I going to teach tomorrow?" I said. Fred, a faith operating "cheerleader", told me that "Faith is action. Healed people go to church." Still feeling awful and weak, I prepared myself for Sunday school and headed for the church. On the way there, the Lord brought into remembrance to me the account of the lepers, who were healed, AS THEY WENT. This encouraged me and I suddenly realized the authority I have in Jesus' Name and I got mad at the devil and rebuked him. Then, I said to myself "If I can just get through Sunday School, I'll be fine." Well, you know what? I was! By the end of Sunday school, I feeling fine...strength restored, all symptoms were gone! Praise God!!!!!

2 Kings 5:1-15 – Naaman, the leper – told to go wash in the Jordan River 7 times. Naaman had to be obedient here. Had he not done what he was told to do, he would not have been healed.

Healing occurs when we use our authority in and say the Name of Jesus.

CHAPTER 6

UNFORGIVENESS

In Jesus' prayer which He taught to His disciples, He tells us to forgive, or, very simply, WE will not be forgiven. Matthew 6:7-15. tells us that we MUST forgive. Romans 2:1 tells us what when we judge or pass sentence on another, we condemn ourselves. Hebrews 12:13 tells us that resentment (bitterness, hatred) causes trouble and bitter torment.

We usually only hear the part of these verses that say: "Have faith in God, tell the mountain to leave and don't doubt and it will happen." But, verse 25 begins with the word 'AND'. The word "AND" means its still part of what came before it. The Word of God goes on to say in verse 25 that "While you're praying, if you remember you have something against someone, you need to forgive them, right then and there, so that God will forgive us our own sins. Notice that this is not "an option" to be done by us out of the goodness of our heart, but rather these are instructions and commands from God.

We MUST forgive, or WE will not be forgiven. John 3:16: "For God so loved the world that He gave His only begotten Son, so that whoever believes in (trusts, clings to, relies on) Him shall not perish but have eternal (everlasting) life."

Romans 5:8 "God shows and clearly proves His (own) love for us by the fact that while we were still sinners, Christ (The Messiah, the anointed One) died for us."

We have been shown mercy by God in His gift to us of eternal life. Jesus paid the price for our sins. It cost us nothing, but to believe Jesus died for us. Forgiveness is offered to us as a free gift by God, through Jesus. We ALL need forgiveness.

In Matthew 10:18 Jesus is again instructing His disciples. He gives them power and authority over unclean spirits, to drive them out and to cure the sick, raise the dead, cleanse the lepers, drive out demons, and He tells them "Freely (without pay) you have received, freely (without charge) give." We have received forgiveness for our many sins. Freely, we need to also forgive those who have sinned against us. You might be thinking to yourself: "Yes, but you don't know...you don't understand what they did to me." You know what?

It really doesn't matter. Sin is sin. It doesn't matter to God. Any unforgiveness on our part can open the door for oppression and depression, and possibly possession. It can open the door for sickness and disease. Unforgiveness causes anger, resentment and bitterness in our emotions. Unresolved emotional issues can cause physical problems, and these can lead, ultimately, to death. So, we can't afford NOT to forgive people. Vengeance should be left to God. Romans 12:19, Deuteronomy 32: 35 & 36; Hebrews 10:30. We must forgive BY FAITH. We don't forget it. Matthew 18:16-34.

Unforgiveness stops prayer, causes sickness, affects your finances. God will deal with you. Matthew 18:23-35. We must forgive.

The same way Joseph had every right and opportunity to be hateful and bitter and unforgiving toward his brothers, so did Daniel. His story is found in the book of Daniel in the Bible. You can read it for yourself. He was captured and taken away from his family and made to serve his conquering king, Nebuchadnezzer. Even so, he struggled to continue to serve his God who had permitted all of this to happen. Daniel didn't get bitter. He got better. He made the best of his situation, with God's help and plan and he rose to infamy. He became a light shining in the darkness. He forgave his captors and chose to move on. And, God used him. Daniel took a tragedy and it became a testimony. Tragedy CAN be followed by greatness. You've been through terrible things, but God can use you to encourage others so they can see how God brought you through. All doesn't have to be a downward spiral. You can be a success in spite of a horrible beginning. God can use you. It's not over till GOD says it's over. God was preparing Daniel for greatness through tragedy. He has a plan for greatness for you too. You don't have to stay in that hell hole you might be in right now. There is a light at the end of the tunnel but you have to do your part. Give your life to God and He will use you for great things. So you've been through a divorce, had an abortion, druggie or boozer...So what!!!! God's not telling you to forget what happened to you, but to forgive them. Face the hurt, forgive it, release it and move on!

In Luke 23:34 – When Jesus was hanging on the cross, filled with unbelievable pain and suffering–He forgave those who had done this to Him. "Then Jesus said "Father, forgive them, for they do not know what they do." So, we need to forgive because Jesus, our sinless example forgave. At the cross, God didn't give us what we deserve. Instead, He gave us what we needed: forgiveness. And God gave us forgiveness because of His Divine mercy.

When we forgive, please realize, we won't forget the situation. God says He remembers our sins no more in Hebrews 10:7. This means that He will never use the past against us. Psalm 103:12.

Forgetting may be a result of forgiving, but it's never the means of forgiving. When we bring up the past to someone, it means that it has not been forgiven. When you don't forgive someone, it means you are still connected to them, and to the pain, the things of the past. We have to let it go, so we can stop the pain of the past and to then be able to walk into the blessed future that God has designed for us. God can't give us a future if we don't let go of the past.

The crowds of people at the cross didn't realize what they were doing. We, on the other hand, choose to do wrong, knowing that the act we are doing is wrong. We ALL need forgiveness. Before we come to God through Jesus, we don't realize we need forgiveness. Our inner spirits need to be so tuned in to God, so that we don't WANT to sin, not because of "sin", but because we love the Lord so much we don't want to hurt Him by our behavior. Forgiveness takes a definite effort on our part, and like love, forgiveness is a choice.

We must forgive ourselves, as well as others. God forgave us. There's no reason for us to keep under self-condemnation. John 8:36 "If the Son makes you free, you shall be free indeed."

We must forgive others.
Matthew 6:7-15; Mark 11:22-26

1 Corinthians 5:17 tells us that if any person is in Christ he is "a new creation (a new creature altogether); The old (previous moral and spiritual condition) has passed away."... that we are made new, not physically, but spiritually.

Matthew 18:23-35 shows us a parable of forgiveness. WE are forgiven for things that we cannot repay, things that we cannot go back and "fix". Verse 35 Jesus says "So also My Heavenly Father will deal with every one of you if you do not freely forgive your brother from your heart his offences." Jesus paid for us a debt He did not owe, a debt we could not pay. We've been forgiven...in turn, we must forgive others. This is also found in Luke 11:1-4.

It's OK to be angry over something, just don't let it control you, so that you sin as a result of it. Ephesians 4:26-27 tells us not to give place to the devil. Paul talks about forgiveness in 2 Corinthians 2:10-11, that we should forgive, so as not to let satan take advantage of us.

If someone had a right to be angry, it was Joseph whose brothers had wanted to kill him. And sold him as a slave which led him to years of an unhappy life. Yet, in Genesis 45:5 & 15, he forgives them. What was meant for evil, God used for good.

Forgiveness includes: Forgiving ourselves, forgiving others and forgiving circumstances.

In Matthew 18:21-35, Peter was asking Jesus how many times he should forgive an offence. Peter, I'm sure thought he was being very generous, suggesting 7 times. Jesus replied 70 times. I believe that could mean 490 times in a day! We must continually forgive. What person, if they really forgave someone, would actually keep a running account of the offenses against them? I feel that if you're keeping a record, you've never really forgiven. If we don't forgive here on earth, we'll suffer the consequences in eternity. Turn from unforgiveness here or burn in hell in the hereafter. Matthew 5:22.

> God requires us to forgive others from our heart or He will turn us over to the tormentors. Matthew 18: 34 & 35.

As Christ forgave you, so you also must do.
Colossians 3:12-13

We must keep our heart tender. An offence can lead to unforgiveness, which can lead to bitterness. Ephesians 4:31-32.

I find in life, that I have enough to do to keep myself in line with God's Word. It's always easier to see someone else's faults, than to see our own. Mind your own business! Take care of yourself. Luke 6:41-42.

Jesus said:

Forgive your enemies Matthew 5:43-48.

Forgive people their trespasses Matthew 6:14-15.

Don't judge others Matthew 7:1-2.

Do for others as you would have them do for you Matthew 7:12.

Let's look at this for a moment from the world's point of view. The medical professionals have discovered that "nursing a grudge is bad for your health." Edward Hallowell, M.D., author of Dare to Forgive says that research reveals that nursing a grudge makes you more prone to back pain, headaches, high blood pressure, stomach aches, even colds and flu. I've read that it's even connected to arthritis and cancer.

Sample Prayer asking for forgiveness for myself And for help for me to forgive others.

HEAVENLY FATHER, I COME TO YOU IN JESUS' NAME; I THANK YOU FOR YOUR LOVING-KINDNESS AND TENDER MERCY TOWARDS ME. I THANK YOU FOR YOUR PATIENCE WITH ME AND ALL MY FAULTS. I THANK YOU THAT I AM YOUR CHILD, AND YOU HAVE FORGIVEN ALL MY SINS. I HAVE NOT DONE THIS TOWARDS THOSE WHO HAVE OFFENDED ME. I HAVE KEPT BITTERNESS AND RESENTMENT TOWARDS THEM INSTEAD. FATHER, PLEASE BRING TO MIND TO ME THOSE PEOPLE I HAVE NOT FORGIVEN SO THAT I CAN FORGIVE THEM. I PRAY THAT YOU ALSO SHOW ME THOSE PEOPLE WHOM I HAVE OFFENDED SO THAT I MAY SEEK FORGIVENESS IN WHATEVER WAY YOU CHOOSE. IN JESUS' NAME. AMEN.

CHAPTER 7

****

TITHES & OFFERINGS

****

What is a tithe? What is an offering? Does a tithe come off "the top" or my income?" Why is this a topic for healing?

TITHE

The Oxford American Dictionary defines a tithe as one-tenth of the annual produce of agriculture, etc. formerly paid as tax to support clergy and church; to contribute one-tenth of one's income to one's church.

NIV Compact Dictionary of the Bible shows the Hebrew word: Maaser, and the Greek Word: Dekate. Both words mean "the tenth".

TITHES & OFFERINGS

No one seems to know for sure when and where the idea arose for making the tenth the rate for paying taxes and tribute to rules and of offering gifts as a religious duty. It does not seem to be recorded. Yet, history shows that it did exist in Babylon in ancient times, as well as in Persia, Egypt, and even in China. Abraham knew of it when he migrated from Ur. Genesis 14:17-20.

Since Melchizedek was a Priest of the Most High, it is certain that by Abraham's day, the giving of tithes had been recognized as a holy act Hebrews 7:1-10. Samuel warned Israel that the king whom they were demanding would exact tithes of their grain and flocks 1 Samuel 8:10-18. When Jacob made his covenant with God at Bethel, it included payment of tithes. Genesis 28:16-22.

It was a long time before definite legal requirements were set on tithing. As a result, customs concerning payment of the tithe varied. At first, the tither was required to share his tithe with the Levites Deuteronomy 14:22-23. After the Levitical code had been completed, tithes then belonged exclusively to the Levites. Numbers 18:21. A penalty of 20% of the tithe was collected from one who sold his tithes and refused to use the money to pay for a substitute. Leviticus 27:31. The Levites, in turn, gave a tenth to provide for the priests. Numbers 18:25-32. The temple was the place to which the tithes were to be taken. Deuteronomy 12:5-12.

To make sure that no dishonesty would occur concerning tithing, each Hebrew was required to make a declaration of his honesty before the Lord. Deuteronomy 26:13-15. This reminds me of when I was a child in grade school. The Catholic elementary schools I attended required that you write "I do so declare" at the end of the test with your signature required afterwards. This was a declaration of honesty as applied to the examination. Interesting.

Was there only one tithe each year, or was the 3RD year tithe an extra one? There is confusion on this question, even among Hebrew scholars. As the need for funds increased to cover the expansion of the temple service, a 3RD year tithe (all for the use of the Levites and those in need) was required.

By the time of Christ, Roman rule had greatly affected the financial life of Judea and it became more and more difficult for people to tithe. But, the laws regarding tithing were still observed in that the Pharisees tithed even herbs, herbs that were used in seasoning food. Matthew 23:23

The tithe is one-tenth of our income. 1/10 or 10% or 10 cents of every dollar. Genesis 14:17-20 Hebrews 7:1-10

The tithe from me, to God, is to come off the "top" of my income. Just look at your paycheck. You have gross salary, and then taxes come out, off the "top". We must give God what is right, not what's left.

The tithe is:
a) Money
b) Things
c) Time

Hebrews 7:4, Matthew 23:23,
Genesis 28:16-22

When we obey God, we're under "the blessing".

When we disobey God, we're under "the curses."

Deuteronomy 11:26-28

Sickness can come because we do not tithe. Malachi 3:8-11 "Will a man rob God? Yet you have robbed Me. But you say, Wherein have we robbed You? In tithes and offerings. You are cursed with a curse; for you have robbed me, even this whole nation. Bring you all the tithes into the storehouse, that there may be meat in My house, and prove Me now herewith, says the Lord of Hosts, if I will not open you the windows of heaven and pour you out a blessing that there shall not be room enough to receive it. And I will rebuke the devourer for your sakes. And he shall not destroy the fruit of your ground; neither shall your vine cast her fruit before the time in the field, says the Lord of Hosts."

OFFERINGS

The Hebrew word for offering is: Zevah; the Greek word is Thysia.

The Oxford American Dictionary definition is: A gift of contribution, etc. that is offered. A presentation or a gift as an act of religious worship.

The NIV Compact Dictionary of the Bible definition is: A religious act belonging to worship in which offering is made to God of some material object belonging to the person. Every offering had to be the honestly acquired property of the offerer. 2 Samuel 24:24.

There were different kinds of offerings:

a) Animals only for sacrifice: i.e. oxen, sheep, goats and pigeons (shedding of blood).
b) Produce of the field: i.e. wine, grain, oil (vegetable or bloodless offering).

The Sin Offering: For sins unconsciously or unintentionally committed—for sins committed deliberately, but with certain circumstances involved. Leviticus 4 & 6. Only the fat was burned completely.

The Guilt or Trespass offering: For sin where restitution or legal satisfaction could be made. Leviticus 5 & 6

The Burnt Offering: Sacrifice was completely consumed on the altar, for the entire consecration of the worshiper to the Lord, for forgiveness. Leviticus 1

The Fellowship or Peace Offering: Was offered by those who were at peace with God, to express gratitude and obligation to God and fellowship with Him. Leviticus 3.

Vegetable or Bloodless Sacrifices

The Grain Offering: Fine flour, unleavened bread, cakes, wafers, ears of grain, toasted, always with salt (possibly corn on the cob) and, except with the sin offering, with olive oil. Leviticus 2 & 6

The Drink Offering: Made in connection with the grain offering that accompanied all burnt offerings and fellowship offerings.

In addition to the blood and bloodless offerings were the:

a) Loaves of showbread found in the Holy Place—replaced every Sabbath.
b) The oil for the 7 branch lamp stand – refilled every morning.
c) The incense for the altar of incense, refilled each morning and evening.

So, what do tithes and offerings mean to us today? The tithe is REQUIRED of us by God. The offering is EVERYTHING above the tithe which we give to God.

I feel that Jesus is our Guilt or Trespass offering. He took our place for sin, where restitution and legal satisfaction had to be made to God. When we receive Jesus as our Savior, He makes Himself to be our substitute, as satisfaction to the Father for our sins, past, present and future.

I feel that it's up to us individually, to consecrate ourselves to God, to confess daily our known and unknown sins and to ask for forgiveness, that when we give our offerings to God, we are expressing our love and gratitude to Him for all His loving kindness and tender mercies to us.

The tithe should be given where we are being spiritually fed....to our home church. Malachi 3 says to "Bring all the tithes into the store house" and that we will be blessed.

The offerings may be given wherever you feel God is directing you. It can go to church, ministry, individual people—just make as sure as you can that your offering is going into <u>BIBLICALLY GOOD GROUND.</u>

We need to have the right attitude in our giving. If you know your attitude is wrong –Don't Give! The Word of God says that God loves a cheerful giver. 2 Corinthians 9:6 -7 tells us that he who "Sows sparingly and grudgingly will also reap grudgingly and sparingly and he who sows generously will also reap generously and with blessings."

The purpose of abundance is so that we can bless God and others. Acts 4:32-35; Acts 6:1 & 2. After all, everything good that we have comes from God. We came naked into this world, and basically other than what we are clothed in by others for burial, we leave here with no earthly possessions.

In Luke 12:16-20, there is the account of the rich man who was keeping all of his money and resources to himself and storing up, probably for his retirement, so he could live comfortably...nothing wrong with that basically. Let's assume that he was tithing to the Lord. That's a good and correct thing. From the way the story is told in the Bible, the man was not generous. He kept planning and planning for the future.

We're told to give to the poor and to share our blessings with the needy, the widow and the homeless. Mark 10:17-23, Luke 6:30-38; Acts 4:32-35; Luke 14:12-14; Acts 6:1-2; Matthew 19:21; Isaiah 58:6-11; 2 Corinthians 9:7; Proverbs 21:13. There are lots more Scriptures on this.

The purpose of having an abundance of money is not just to pamper ourselves, but it's so that we can help others less fortunate than ourselves and to be able to give "good gifts". Luke 14:13; Luke 18:22; John 13:2, 9; Galatians 2:10; Matthew 7:11; Luke 11:13.

It's not wrong to want to have money. It's the LOVE of money that's wrong. 1 Timothy 6:10. We shouldn't be consumed with making and having money that it becomes our number one focus. We're told not to worry about having food, clothing and our needs met. God knows we have basic needs and He provides for us.

We're told to trust God for all our needs. 1 Peter 5:7, Philippians 4:6, Matthew 6:28, Luke 12:27. We need to place our faith in God. Did you know that anything not faith is sin? It's true. To worry is to tell God that He's not big enough or powerful enough to take care of us.

Giving is like planting a seed into the Kingdom of God. When it comes down to it, only what we do to serve God is lasting. When we leave this earth, we leave with no earthly possessions. Whatever we leave behind most likely, will be fought over by our relatives. It's probably not so much that you've died and they'll miss you, but "What did he leave me?" In many many families greed comes out when someone dies. It can even wreck family relationships. I've seen it happen. Of course, there are exceptions to this and everything is done peacefully and with respect for one another. All that you've scrimped and saved for all your life will be sold and spent on the "goodies" of life. People spend thousands of dollars in weeks. God's no fool. He knows what His children are like, so He tells us to be generous and give it away.

Bruce Wilkinson, in his book A Life that God Rewards, gives a good analogy. He states that our whole life is like "a dot" – we're really here in this life a short time compared to eternity. Eternity is represented by a long, unending drawn line. We need to live our lives with the line in mind, not the dot. Giving is one example of living for "the line."

We must be willing to give our offering and then our gift is acceptable. We are to give according to what we have, not according to what we don't have. God doesn't want us to be unfairly burdened with our offerings. We're to share our surplus with others so that at some point others may share their surplus at our point of need. 11 Corinthians 8:12-14.

Let everyone give willingly as we feel in our heart and not under any duress, but sincerely wanting

IN YOUR FACE devil TAKIN' BACK MY STUFF

to give. He who sows sparingly will reap sparingly. 11 Corinthians 9:6-12.

God will bless and reward us for our giving, not only monetarily but God will bestow favor upon us, favor from Him, given to us through mankind. Giving is a sign of our thanks to God for all He's done for us.

CHAPTER 8

WORDS SPOKEN

Mark 11:22-25: "And Jesus replying said to them, Have faith in God. Truly I tell you, whoever says to this mountain be lifted up and thrown into the sea! And does not doubt at all in his heart but believes that what he says will take place; it will be done for him. For this reason I am telling you whatever you ask for in prayer, believe (trust and be confident) that it is granted to you and you will get it and whenever you stand praying, if you have anything against anyone, forgive him and let it drop. (Leave it, let it go) in order that your Father who is in heaven may also forgive you your (own) failings and shortcomings and let them drop."

The words that we speak and hear are so very important, every day of our lives. They affect us either positively or negatively.

Proverbs 18:21. What we continually hear with our ears, eventually, we believe and, eventually, if we hear them often enough, they become fact in our life. They become reality Matthew 12:37; Proverbs 21:23; Proverbs 18:21 "Death and life are in the power of the tongue and they who indulge in it shall eat the fruit of it (death or life)." Matthew 12:37 "For by your words you will be justified, and by your words you will be condemned and sentenced.

Proverbs 21:23 "He who guards his mouth and his tongue keeps himself from troubles."

We must maintain a good confession. Most people think that when you use the word "confessions", that it means confessing sin or something bad they've done. And, this is true sometimes. But the confession we're discussing here is right talking or speaking right, wholesome, positive things. It's not enough just to believe something is going to happen. We have to speak it out. That means using our mouth to say it so that our ears and our spirit man and the devil can hear it.

Romans 10:9, 10 & 17 states that if you acknowledge and confess with your lips that Jesus is Lord and in your heart believe that God raised Him from the dead, you will be saved. With their heart a person believes and is justified, AND, with their mouth confesses and confirms salvation. The Word of God states that faith comes by hearing and what is heard comes by the preaching of Christ.

In the same way, we have to continually hear the Word of God, continually hear the Scriptures which promise us healing and whatever else we need, but we must also speak things out ourselves, so that our faith will build for these things and we will become convinced that the need will be met and then our bodies will come into line with what the Word of God promises us was already accomplished when Jesus died on the cross and God raised Him from the dead.

Everyone is not on the same faith level. God meets us where we are. Use what you know. Do what you know to do. Speak out your healing. Do it in private. People probably already think you're crazy because you read your Bible and go to church and you're one of "those people"...And, if you say stuff like "HALLELUJAH!" and "PRAISE THE LORD." That REALLY proved to them that you're weird.

Jesus accomplished for me everything I need, here and now in this life,

I don't deny the symptoms. I must use my faith to speak out my healing.

I'm not moved by what I see. I'm moved by what the Word of God says about me.

I am what God says I am.

I have what God says I have.

I can do what God says I can do.
Retrain: Your brain to think positively.
Retrain: Your mouth to speak positively.

Distraught Thoughts (taken from Inspiration Daily on the computer)
If you keep saying you're always broke, guess what? You'll always be broke.
If you keep saying you can't find a job, you will remain unemployed.
If you keep saying you can't trust a man or trust a woman, you will always find someone in your like to hurt and betray you.
If you keep saying you can't find someone to love you or believe in you, your very thoughts will attract more experiences to confirm your beliefs.
Turn your thoughts and conversations around to be more positive and power packed with faith, hope and action. Don't be afraid to believe that you can have what you want and deserve.
Watch your thoughts, they become words. Watch your words, they become actions. Watch your actions, they become habits. Watch your habits, they become character. Watch your character, for it becomes your destiny. Reread Charles Capps' Positive Daily Confession starting on page 57 of this book.... Use it daily.

CHAPTER 9

****

GENERATIONAL CURSES

****

Galatians 3:13 states that "Christ has redeemed us from the curse of the law, being made a curse for us; for it is written cursed is everyone that hangs on a tree."

> Jeremiah 32:18: "(God shows) loving-kindness to thousands but recompenses the iniquity of the fathers into the bosoms of their children after them. So, curses are real.

> Deuteronomy 27-30 contains blessings and curses. Moses read these to the people. Jesus redeemed us from the curses brought on us by our sins. Galatians 3:13 So, in this life, we're either under the blessing or under the curse. To protect ourselves from the curse, we just walk in obedience to the Word of God.

Sin opens the door for curses to come into our lives. Jesus redeemed us from the curse, so, it's already been done. But then again, He died for our salvation as well, and everything else we need in the sometimes nasty here and now AND in the sweet by and by. We each need to receive them for ourselves. They don't come automatically. We must each receive Jesus' death and atonement for sin for ourselves. The same way, we must each receive our own personal healing, our own personal prosperity and redemption from curses. We must do things God's way because God is sovereign.

Jesus said that He had some to earth to set us free from: sin, emotional pain and illness, physical afflictions... Isaiah 61:1-3, to comfort our mourning and give us praise instead. Matthew 4:23, Luke 4:16-21, and to proclaim the year of the Lord.

His mission to earth has still not changed. He still wants to set you free from sin so you can go to your real home in Heaven. He still wants to heal you of emotional pain and illness and He still wants to comfort you and set you free from mourning and He still proclaims the year of the Lord. In His own words, He came to set the captives free.

Captivity can mean any number of things:

Poverty, Emotional/mental illness, worry, sickness and disease, pride, relationship/ divorce issues, addictions, negative words spoken against you, witchcraft/control issues.

There are many kinds of curses and, as many as there are of these curses, there are many reasons that they may come upon us.

Proverbs 6:2 states "The curse causeless shall not come."

Deuteronomy 21:22-23 "Any sin worthy of death is also cursed by God."

Numbers 14:18 tells us "The Lord is longsuffering, and of great mercy, forgiving iniquity and transgression, and by no means clearing the guilty using the iniquity of the fathers upon the children until the third and fourth generation."

Other Scriptures: Exodus 20:3-5; Exodus 34:7; Jeremiah 32:18; Lamentations 5:7; Ezekiel 18; Ezekiel 20:27-30; Leviticus 26:40; Nehemiah 9:2, 16; John 9:1-3.

It's my understanding that a generation is considered to be anywhere from 25-40 years –That would make the curse last for 160 years. I've also read that a curse lasts for 400 years. At any rate, that's a long time, and none of us would know what happened 160 or 400 years ago with our ancestors.

So, what is a curse anyway?

According to Oxford American Dictionary, Oxford University Press, 1980, a curse is defined as

"A call for evil to come upon a person or thing; the evil produced by this; a violent exclamation of anger; something that causes evil or harm."

According to NIV Compact Dictionary of the Bible, Zondervan Publishing House, a curse is: "The reverse of "to bless". On the human level: to wish harm or catastrophe; on the divine level: to impose judgment. To the Oriental mind, the curse carried with it its own power of execution. The modern Western practice of cursing, i.e. using profane language is never referred to in the Scriptures."

The first generational curse was handed down to us by Adam and Eve. They disobeyed God back in the Garden of Eden and so it began. As a result of Adam and Eve's sin, we are born sinners! Adam and Eve's son, Cain, was the first murderer. Lamech became the second murderer. Genesis 4:8, 23…and so on, and so on. The family curse can be a sickness or disease, mental illness, drugs, alcohol, divorce, eating disorders, anger, poverty, dying before your time, child abuse. Think about it. In our own society today we look at the Kennedy family and all the tragedies that have hit them over the years and we describe it as the "Kennedy curse". Even the Boston Red Socks baseball team was known for having a losing curse on them until they won in 2004. Curses are real! Even in the natural, there are the expressions:

    1) What goes around comes around.
    2) The apple doesn't fall far from the tree.
    3) You're just like your father/mother.

and these sayings refer to behaviors, either ours or someone in our family or someone we know about. No one plans to be an alcoholic or addicted to drugs, an abuser, to divorce multiple times, become mentally ill, get cancer, heart disease or diabetes. These things are generational. Don't despair. They can be stopped. When Jesus died He died not only for our sins, but He died to set you free from the family curses. When the Son sets you free, you're free indeed, but someone has to take the initiative to break the curse. While it's already done, just like salvation is, it has to be received personally as well. But even better, you can break the curse over yourself and over your children and future children as well. And, you can speak a blessing over your family.

No amount of good behavior, sorrow, or good intentions can bring release from the curses of the law. It requires an eye for an eye, a tooth for a tooth. The law must be satisfied, and the the penalty carried out in full. God punishes disobedience and rewards righteousness and faith. Romans 2:9-11; Galatians 6:7; Ephesians 6:8; Revelation 13:10.

Romans 2:9-11 "Tribulation and anguish upon every soul of man that doeth evil, of the Jew first and also of the gentile; but glory, honor and peace to every man that worketh good, to the Jew first and also to the Gentile, for there is no respect of persons with God." We always hear what's said in verse 11: "God is not a respecter of persons". But, we don't hear those two verses before, especially the one that speaks of tribulation, calamity and anguish on the one who does evil.

Galatians 6:7 "Don't be deceived, for God is not mocked; for what a man sows, that also shall he reap."

Ephesians 6:8 "What good thing man does, the same he shall receive of the Lord."

Revelation 13:10 "He that leads into captivity shall go into captivity; he that kills with the sword must be killed by the sword."

Recently I was at a service where the speaker explained the difference between "sin" and "iniquity". I had always thought they were the same, interchangeable words for the same thing. But, they're not. Sin is missing the mark, the act that I commit. On the other hand, iniquity, is that driving force within me that makes me want to sin. So, get rid of the iniquity, the driving force causing it and sin will no longer be there. We have to close the door on it and keep it closed. Matthew 12:43-45

Curses are upon nations, as well as individuals.

Slavery produced prejudice and bigotry. Bigotry produces discrimination and abuse of people.

Rape produces rape
Abortion produces abortion
Illegal Drugs produces illegal drugs

Perversions produce homosexuals

The good news is: Galatians 3:13: "Christ has redeemed us from the curse of the law, being made a curse for us." and Galatians 5:8 "Those who are walking the Spirit are above the law."

All the benefits of the cross must be received by faith.

James 4:3 says: "Ye have not because ye ask not."

In order to break curses against ourselves, We need to:

Be born again. John 3:7. Come to God through Jesus. Apply the Blood of Jesus to our lives. Our sins are washed away and we're clean as if we've never committed them, as if we've never sinned.

Acknowledge the problem, through the Holy Spirit. Let the Holy Spirit reveal the problem to us. Recognize it for what it is.

Ask God to forgive the forefathers and ancestors involved, whether dead or alive. If we've also involved, ask God for personal forgiveness. Be specific. Ask for specific forgiveness for specific sins.

Break the curse using our spiritual weapons. 2 Corinthians 10:4. Our weapons are not of the flesh but from God. Ephesians 6:10-13. The person is not your enemy. We have a spiritual enemy. Use the armor of God. Don't ever take it off. Ephesians 6:14-17.

Apart from Jesus and His Blood, we can't be free from anything. We can't free ourselves from inside a paper bag!

Proclaim the Name of Jesus. Luke 10:19; Isaiah 54:17

Ask the Lord to show you any inroad that a curse may have come into your life. Proverbs 26:2

Repent of any known sin, or bitterness.

In the Name of Jesus, command the power of the curse to be broken Psalm 19 back to its roots. Destroy the curse on both sides of the family and every legal hold and every legal ground.

The following is a sample of Curse Breaking:

I BREAK EVERY CURSE OPERATING AGAINST ME AND MY FAMILY LINE IN THE AREA OF_____, IN JESUS' NAME. YOU CAN DO THIS FOR YOUR CHILDREN AS WELL.

Thank God for His forgiveness and believe for miracles.

Prayer of Deliverance

HEAVENLY FATHER, I REPENT OF ALL SINS IN MY LIFE OR MY ANCESTORS' LIVES THAT RESULTED IN A CURSE. I REPENT OF ALL DISOBEDIENCE, REBELLION, PERVERSION, WITCHCRAFT, IDOLATRY, LUST, ADULTERY, FORNICATION, MISTREATMENT OF OTHERS, MURDER, CHEATING, LYING, SORCERY,

DIVINATION AND OCCULT INVOLVEMENT AND ASK FOR FORGIVENESS AND GENERATIONAL CLEANSING THROUGH THE BLOOD OF JESUS CHRIST. I TAKE AUTHORITY OVER AND BREAK EVERY CURSE UPON MY LIFE, GENERATIONAL CURSES IN THE NAME OF JESUS. I BREAK ALL CURSES OF POVERTY, LACK, DEBT, DESTRUCTION, SICKNESS, DEATH AND VAGABOND. I BREAK ALL CURSES ON MY MARRIAGE, FAMILY, CHILDREN AND RELATIONSHIPS. I BREAK CURSES OF REJECTION, PRIDE, REBELLION, LUST, HURT, INCEST, RAPE, AHAB, JEZEBEL, FEAR, INSANITY, MADNESS AND CONFUSION. I BREAK ALL CURSES AFFECTING MY FINANCES, MIND, SEXUAL CHARACTER, EMOTIONS, WILL AND RELATIONSHIPS. I BREAK EVERY HEX, JINX, SPELL AND SPOKEN CURSE OVER MY LIFE. I BREAK EVERY FETTER, SHACKLE, CHAIN, CORD, HABIT AND CYCLE THAT IS THE RESULT OF A CURSE. GALATIANS 3:13 SAYS I HAVE BEEN REDEEMED FROM THE CURSE OF THE LAW BY THE SACRIFICE OF JESUS. I USE MY FAITH NOW IN THE BLOOD OF JESUS AND LOOSE MYSELF AND MY DECENDANTS FROM EVERY CURSE. I RECEIVE FORGIVENESS THROUGH THE BLOOD OF JESUS FOR THE SINS OF THE FATHERS. ALL MY SINS HAVE BEEN FORGIVEN AND I LOOSE MYSELF FROM THE CURSE THAT CAME AS A RESULT OF ALL DISOBEDIENCE AND REBELLION

TO THE WORD OF GOD. I CONFESS THAT ABRAHAM'S BLESSINGS ARE MINE. I AM NOT CURSED, BUT BLESSED. I AM THE HEAD AND NOT THE TAIL. I AM ABOVE AND NOT BENEATH. I AM BLESSED COMING IN AND GOING OUT. I AM BLESSED AND WHAT GOD HAS BLESSED CANNOT BE CURSED. I COMMAND SPIRITS OF REJECTION, HURT, BITTERNESS, UNFORGIVENESS, BONDAGE, TORMENT, DEATH, DESTRUCTION, FEAR, LUST, PERVERSION, MIND CONTROL, WITCH-CRAFT, POVERTY, LACK, DEBT, CONFUSION, DOUBLE MINDEDNESS, SICKNESS, INFIRMITY, PAIN, DIVORCE, SEPARATION, STRIFE, CONTENTION, DEPRESSION, SADNESS, LONELINESS, SELF-PITY, SELF-DESTRUCTION, SELF REJECTION, ANGER, RAGE, WRATH, ANGUISH, VAGABOND, ABUSE AND ADDICTION TO <u>COME OUT</u> IN THE NAME OF JESUS CHRIST, THE POWER OF HIS SHED BLOOD AND THE MINISTRY AND POWER OF THE HOLY GHOST. LORD, I THANK YOU FOR SETTING ME FREE FROM EVERY CURSE AND EVERY SPIRIT THAT HAS OPERATED IN MY LIFE AS THE RESULT OF A CURSE. IN JESUS' NAME, AMEN.

Special prayer of protection over children:

I TAKE AUTHORITY OVER YOU SATAN IN THE NAME OF JESUS CHRIST, AND RENDER YOU POWERLESS IN THE LIFE OF _____

_____ (CHILD'S NAME) I BIND YOUR POWER, BREAK YOUR INFLUENCE, AND LOOSE _____ (CHILD'S NAME) FROM YOUR GRIP. ALL HARMFUL HEREDITARY AND ANY OTHER SPIRITS. I BREAK IN THE NAME OF JESUS, AND BY FAITH I NOW TAKE THE BLOOD OF JESUS AND CLEANSE THE CONSCIOUS MIND, THE SUB-CONSCIOUS MIND, THE EMOTIONS, THE IMAGINATIONS, THE HEART AND WILL OF _____ (NAME CHILD) I THANK YOU FOR THE POWER AND AUTHORITY OF YOUR NAME AND BLOOD, LORD JESUS, AND ASK YOU TO KEEP THE HEART OF_____ (NAME CHILD), OPEN AND TENDER TO THE LEADING OF THE HOLY SPIRIT. PLEASE FILL _____ (CHILD'S NAME) WITH YOUR EVERLASTING LOVE, YOUR PEACE, AND YOUR JOY, FOR YOUR GLORY. I ASK THIS IN THE NAME OF JESUS. AMEN.

Open doors that can cause generational curses:

Those who curse or mistreat Jews.
> Genesis 12:3; Genesis 27:29,
> Deuteronomy 27:26; Numbers 24:9

Those that deliberately deceive.
> Genesis 27:12; Joshua 9:23,
> Jeremiah 48:10; Malachi 1:14

An adulterous woman.   Numbers 5:27

Disobedience to the Lord's Commandments.
Deuteronomy 11:28;
Daniel 9:11, Jeremiah 11:3

Idolatry (Anything that comes before God).
Exodus 20:5, Deuteronomy 5:8-9,
Deuteronomy 29:19, Jeremiah 44:8

Those who keep or own cursed objects.
Deuteronomy 7:25; Joshua 6:18

Those that refuse to come to the Lord's help.
Judges 5:23

House of the wicked.   Proverbs 3:33

He who does not give to the poor.
Proverbs 28:27

The earth by reason of man's disobedience.
Isaiah 24:3-6

Jerusalem is a curse to all nations if Jews
rebel against God.   Jeremiah 26:6

Thieves and those who swear falsely by the
Lord's Name.   Zechariah 5:4

Ministers who fail to give the glory to God.
Malachi 3:9; Revelation 1:6

Those who rob God of tithes and offerings.
Haggai 1:6-9; Malachi 3:9

Those who listen to their wives rather than God. Genesis 3:17

Those who lightly esteem their parents.
Deuteronomy 27:16

Those that make graven images.
Exodus 20:4; Deuteronomy 5:8;
Deuteronomy 27:15

Those that deliberately cheat people out of their property. Deuteronomy 27:18

Those who take advantage of the blind
Deuteronomy 27:18

Those who oppress strangers, widows or fatherless.
Exodus 22:22-24; Deuteronomy 27:19

Him who has sex with his father's wife.
Deuteronomy 27:20

Him who has sex with any beast.
Exodus 22:19;
Deuteronomy 27:21

Him who has sex with his sister.
Deuteronomy 27:22

We have a free will and need to make good decisions. We are weak, but Jesus is strong.
Ephesians 3:20, Romans 8:37

Now this list of curses may not apply to you. But remember, a generational curse can go back 40 years or more, so who knows what your ancestors did?

Forgive those who've hurt you. Matthew 6:12 & 15. Matthew 5:44. Forgive as Jesus forgave. Luke 23:34. People are not your enemy, satan is. Forgive so you won't be bitter. Hebrews 12:15. The bottom line is that hurt people, hurt people....and, forgive YOURSELF.

CHAPTER 10

```
********************************************
```

FAITH

```
********************************************
```

Amplified Bible: – Hebrews 11:1 "Now faith is the assurance (the confirmation, the title deed) of the things (we hope for, being the proof of things (we) do not see and the conviction of their reality (faith perceiving as real fact what is not revealed to the senses)."

Hebrews 11:6: "But without faith it is impossible to please and be satisfactory to Him. For whoever would come near to God must (necessarily) believe that God exists and that He is the Rewarder of those who earnestly and diligently seek Him (out)."

Hebrews 12:2: Tells us that we must look away from all that will distract us and look to Jesus, who is the source of our faith.

FAITH is believing something you can't see, that something unseen is in place and is going to happen, that it's a reality, though you can't understand it. We live by faith every day: When we turn the light switch on in our home, that the light will go on. When we turn the faucet on at home, that water will flow. When we insert the car key into the ignition of our car and turn, that, all things considered—we expect the engine to start. We pick up the phone receiver at home, turn on our cell phones, and prepare to make a phone call, we expect the phone to work and the call will go through. We turn on the TV, CD, DVD, and VIDEO —- and expect these electronic machines to perform for us. When I'm making a purchase at a department store, and I hand the cashier my credit card, I expect the sale to go through, as if I had a fistful of cash in my hand.

I don't understand how any of this technical, electronic equipment works—I really don't care—They just work.

We step out of our beds in the morning and expect the floor to hold up. We don't first pray: "Dear God, let this floor hold me." No. We expect it to happen. For those of you who go to amusement parks and put yourself on really fast rides that whip you around in carts, turning you upside down and sideways...You expect that you'll be safe and not fall out to your death. THAT'S FAITH!!!

Why do we have so much trouble having faith in God? Simply put, we don't trust God. Why don't we trust God?

We don't know Him.
We don't know what His Word says.
We don't believe Him.
We don't love Him.
We refuse to do things God's Way.
We don't spend time with God, to get to know
    His Heart.
We have fear.

We've all been given a measure of faith. Romans 12:3 What we do with our faith determines whether that faith increases or decreases. Romans 10:17 says that Faith comes by hearing, continuous hearing of the Word of God. Faith comes, so the opposite applies as well, faith leaves. Faith comes by hearing the Word of God. Faith leaves by not hearing the Word of God. It's that simple.

Your spiritual faith is something that grows by using what you've been given, and then seeing that God has been faithful and trustworthy to do what His Word says He'll do. Simply, faith is believing God. Faith is based on the knowledge of what God has said, and first hand experience of the reliability of God. Isaiah 5:13; Hosea 4:6; Ephesians 4:18. The bottom line, I believe, to faith, is that God wants us to trust Him, to believe Him that He'll do what He says He'll do. Jesus is our source of faith. So, when we believe God and have Jesus as our Savior, we also have the

133

faith the God requires of us in order to please Him. God has made the requirement—Have faith in Me, believe Me. Jesus has given us the necessary faith. Our part is to use the faith we already have. We need to speak out audibly what God says we have, that we are who God says we are, that we can do what God says we can do.

Let me give you some examples of faith in the Bible. The way I see it, there are several kinds of faith: no faith, little faith, great faith and faith in action.

NO FAITH

Mark 4:35-41. The apostles and Jesus were in a boat. A major storm arose and they were fearful and awoke Jesus. He rebuked the storm and asked them "How is it that you have no faith?"

Mark 16. The disciples didn't believe Mary Magdalene had seen Jesus after He had risen from the dead, nor did they believe the two that Jesus met on the road to Emmaus. Jesus reproached and reproved his disciples for their unbelief, lack of faith.

LITTLE FAITH

Matthew 16:5-12. Jesus rebukes His disciples for their little faith after they had seen Him feed thousands twice with only a few loaves of bread.

Matthew 17:14-21. Jesus told His disciples they could not cast out a demon in a boy due to their littleness of faith (but this kind of demon also needed prayer and fasting).

Matthew 14:22. Right after the feeding of the 5,000 men, Peter walked on the water with what Jesus called "little faith".

GREAT FAITH

Matthew 5:22-28. Referring to a woman from Tyre/Sidon pleading for healing for her demon possessed daughter.

Luke 7:2-10. A centurion came to Jesus seeking healing for his servant. Jesus was going to go with him, but the man told Jesus that he was unworthy, for Him to only speak and he knew it would be done. Jesus marveled at the great faith of this man.

Rahab the harlot is mentioned as having great faith in Hebrews 11. James 2 also mentions her. Jesus was born out of her lineage.

FAITH IN ACTION

In these accounts you will find the phrase "Your faith has made you whole." This is faith in action.

Matthew 9:1-8: A man on a sleeping mat lowered down through a hole they made in a roof to get their friend to Jesus. It was the friends' faith in action.

Mark 5: 25-34: A woman with an issue of blood for many years worked her way through a crowd to Jesus to touch the hem of his garment, expecting her healing.

Mark 10:46-52/Luke 19:35-43: The blind beggar, Bartimaeus, was healed.

Luke 7:37-50 Mary Magdelene poured oil on Jesus' head and feet. Jesus said "Your faith has saved you".

Luke 17:12-19: 10 lepers were healed, "as they went".

John 4: 46-51, 53: A royal officer whose son was ill was told his son had died as he spoke with Jesus. Jesus told him to go in peace that his son will live. The man put his trust (faith and belief) in what Jesus said and started home. As he was still on the road his servants met him and told him his son was alive!

The Bible tells us that it's impossible to please God without faith. As a contrasting study, look at the accounts of Zachariah being told of the coming birth of John the Baptist and Mary the young virgin who would be the mother of Jesus in Luke 1:5-80. Zachariah had doubt concerning what the angel Gabriel told him, while Mary believed the angel. We need to learn to doubt your doubts and to stand firm on God's Word. Faith comes by hearing and by using it.

1 Peter 1:6 & 7 tells us that the purpose of trials, tests, temptations and persecutions is to test our faith and to test the genuineness of our faith.

Ecclesiastes 7:14 tells us that adversity will come that we look within.

D Martyn Lloyd-Jones, former pastor of London's Westminster Chapel said: "Faith is holding on to the faithfulness of God, and, as long as you do that, you cannot go wrong. Faith does not look at itself or at the person who is exercising it. Faith looks at God. Faith is interested in God only, and it talks about God and it praises God and it extols the virtues of God. The measure of the strength of a man's faith, always, is ultimately the measure of his knowledge of God...He knows God so well that he can rest on the knowledge. And it is the prayers of such a man that are answered."

CHAPTER 11

PRAISE & WORSHIP

What is praise?

The NIV Compact Dictionary of the Bible defines praise as: "A general term for words or deeds that exalts or honor men, women, heathen gods or God, especially in song (glorious deeds, glory)." Some of the Hebrew and Greek words mean virtue (arête) "thanksgiving, blessing, or glory"—also translated "praises" or "excellences". We are to be the praise of God's glory—Praise fills the Book of Psalms, increasing in intensity toward the end. Psalms 113-118 are called the Hallel, the Praises. Praise for redemption dominates the New Testament.

Praise, According to Webster's Dictionary includes:

Commending, expressing approval, favorable judgment of, glorifying, crediting with perfections. Commend to, entrust for care or preservation, worthy of confidence or notice, approve to have or express a favorable opinion, to show esteem. glorify, to bestow honor, praise, and admiration.

What is worship? The same publication defines Worship as "The honor, reverence, and homage paid to superior beings or powers, whether men, angels, or God. The English word "worthship" means and denotes the worthiness of the individual.

It seems to me that in our church services today, that the fast, lively music with song, dance and hand-clapping, must be the praise, while the slower, more serious songs seem to be considered worship. God has a plan and a purpose for everything.

Praise and worship are acts by which we each make a definite decision to do. They flow out of a life that is grateful to God for all He has done in their lives—out of a life that genuinely loves God. We will not always "feel" like praising God. We should not let our emotions have the final word on whether or not we praise God. When we're upset, we won't "feel" like praising God. When we're angry, we don't "feel" like praising God. We must "cast down imaginations", put down the negative thinking that's mentioned in 2 Corinthians 10:5, and cause our thoughts to come under the authority of Christ—cause every human thought to surrender in obedience to Christ.

When you force yourself to praise God, then it becomes, in my opinion, a "sacrifice of praise", because I, me, the human part really doesn't always want to do it. It's a decision. "I will" praise God. "I will" give thanks to God. "I will" sing to the Lord. Just as satan had his "I will" statements, we need to have ours, only positive ones towards God. In Hebrews 13:15. it talks about the sacrifice of praise as the "fruit of our lips."

When you CHOOSE to open your mouth and to praise God, the spiritual atmosphere changes...GOD arrives on the scene! The "fruit of our lips" doesn't mean silent praise that's in your head. It has to come out of your mouth, audibly. It's not so much that God needs to hear it. It's that you and I need to hear ourselves praising God. Faith comes by hearing, and hearing, and hearing, and hearing and hearing. You get the idea. Praise is the highest form of showing faith in God.

How can we praise someone we don't know? Well, we get to know earthly people by spending time with them. It's no different with God. We get to know God by spending time with Him. Learn what His own Word says about Him. What kinds of things did He do in the Word? Look at His mighty, awesome power shown in the Word. Look for His characteristics. He's all powerful—drove back the sea, made it stand up with the breath of His nostrils! More than once, the Israelites walked across water on dry ground. He floated an ax head. He multiplied loaves and fish, not once, but TWICE. He opened up the ground and swallowed up a man, his whole family and all they possessed and then closed up the ground. This is a POWERFUL God!!!

Do you really realize who He us and Who we're refusing to praise and worship? I challenge you to see who God is. Get to know Him like you know your favorite person's likes and dislikes. How we praise shows how well we know Him. Praise and worship to God should be a daily affair, not reserved only for church days. Praise should be part of our every day life, just as prayer and time in the Word. Part of our daily focus should always be on God. We need to put Him first in our lives, even if it means rearranging our schedules.

How do we praise God? Praise Him, first, for who He is. Use His Names to praise Him. Go through the letters of the alphabet and bring His Names to memory that way. Psalm 100:4

Praise Him for all His creative, marvelous works, for making the earth, animals, and us. The Word tells us marvelous are His creations. Psalm 139:14.

Say grace before meals and thank Him for His provision for us.

Thank Him for His protection.

Praise God by telling someone what God did for you today. It gets tiring hearing what God did for you 20 years ago. Psalm 126:1-3

Praise God at home, in your car, privately, just you and Him. Have church in your car!

Don't complain about things or people. Praise God for positive things instead.

Ephesians 5:19 & 20

Lift your voice and sing and pray in English, and pray and sing in the Spirit.

Psalm 66:8, 98:4-6, Acts 10:46;
1 Corinthians 14:2 & 15.

Clap your hands to the wonderful music, praising God. Praise and worship should always be active within us. The Praise & Worship Team is not there to drag it out of you. It's our choice whether or not to praise God. Psalm 47:1, Isaiah 55:12

Shout for joy to the Lord! Who cares who's listening! Psalm 98:4; Psalm 35:27

Stand up and praise God.

Nehemiah 9:5; 1 Chronicles 23:30

Kneel before the Lord.

Psalm 95:6; Philippians 2:10 & 11

Dance before the Lord.

Psalm 149:3, Psalm 150:4

Lift up your hands to the Lord.

Psalm 63:4; Psalm 134; 1 Timothy 2:8

Praise God with musical instruments.
2 Samuel 6:5; Psalm 150

God wants our love and our praise. He isn't moved by our tears. God isn't moved by our long, elegant prayers. God is moved by faith. Faith moves God. We need to create an atmosphere of faith and trust in God. Welcome Him into your heart and home. God has a special plan and purpose for us and for our lives.   Romans 8:28; Jeremiah 29:11.

Why praise God?

Because you believe in Him, love Him, and want to please Him.
Because you want to honor Him and obey Him.
Because we can't live spiritually or physically without Him.
Because there are things in this world over which we have no control.
Because He's always been faithful to you.
Because of His promises to you in His Word.
Because we want His Presence.

WORSHIP

A worshiper loves God and wants to be with Him as much as possible. A worshiper has a passion for God. Psalm 42:1 & 2. A worshiper truly wants to know God and to obey Him. Worship brings God's Presence. Worship is

God responding to our praise. We need to ask God for His Presence. True worshipers spend hours in God's Presence, and that's a requirement they set for their lives. We need to choose God.

Psalm 24:15; Psalm 9:10; Psalm 14:2

God rewards those who diligently seek Him. Hebrews 11:6. Worship is the end result of praise.

We need to seek God with our praise and worship until He blesses us with His Presence.

Habakkuk 2:20; 2 Chronicles 5:13 & 14.

God's Presence brings:

Joy: Psalm 16:11;
Rest: Matthew 11:29; Peace: John 14:27;
Blessings: Genesis 39:2; Psalm 65:4;
The right people: 2 Samuel 2:30;
Power: Romans 16:20; Psalm 91:9-16;
    1 Corinthians 15:24; Malachi 4:2 & 3;
satan's defeat: 2 Corinthians 10:4;
    1 Corinthians 14:15; 1 John 3:8;
Wisdom: Psalm 111:10; Healing.

Since I first wrote this chapter, I've come to learn more. True worship is not music, but living a righteous life. True worship of God is living a life of obedience to Him and correct living. You can praise & worship God without music. Just use your own words to speak to your Heavenly Daddy. Let your heart speak for you. Just let your words come out of your heart.

These things come out of loving God. If I love you, in the natural, I want to please you all the time. I want to spend all my time with you, do everything I can for you. I want to help you if you need something. I dress to please you, put on my make up or fix my hair to look nice for you...put perfume on to smell good for you...make you the cookies you like from scratch though store bought ones would be easier. The natural is a reflection of the supernatural.

If I say I love God and I appreciate Him, then I read and study His Word. I talk to Him in prayer using every day words. I do things to please Him. How do I know what pleases Him? Read His Word, the Bible. His Word is His will. Do what He says to do, love the things He loves, hate the things He hates. John Bevere in his book Drawing Near gives us good instruction in this area. True worship comes out of obedience to God. True faith produces obedience.

Romans 1:5: The Book of James tells us that faith without works (deeds, obedience) is dead.

Praise and worship is the main activity in Heaven. We can see this when we read the Book of Revelation. As believers on earth, this is also to be our function here on earth. Sometimes healing and deliverance occurs during times of worship. Our praise is to be in thanksgiving for our redemption. There's no greater gift that we could have – the great mercy of our God – We're forgiven!!!!

I just finished watching part of a conference TV program with Tommy Tenney. He was speaking about having a passion for God. As I watched, tears started to stream down my face. Yes, I believe I've finally found my main purpose in life...to worship God! Anything else is secondary in my life. What do I really love? To worship God. I wish I could always be in the Presence of God.

CHAPTER 12

WARFARE LANGUAGE

****

My husband and I have been through some spiritual warfare training and actual hands on since I last wrote these next two chapters. It's made me rethink them. We wage warfare, but not against flesh and blood, but against the unholy spirit rhelm. 2 Corinthians 10:3-6 and Ephesians 6:12. Spiritual warfare is not to be entered into lightly. You must first be sure that you are born again and filled with the Holy Spirit. You must be sure that you have a daily walk with God and that you're constantly trying to keep your life clean and pure. There's an account in the Bible of the sons of Sceva, who, in Acts 19:13-17 got beat up for their improper efforts at casting out demons. This is serious. This could happen to you. Deliverance is not a game. Those who are involved in deliverance ministry are attacked spiritually more than other people.

I strongly suggest that if you feel you are demonically oppressed, that you seek out Christians who are filled with the Holy Spirit and trained in this regard.

James 1:5 "What one needs to do the work God gives him, will surely be given."

Create an atmosphere of praise and worship and thanksgiving.

Everything, always, always, always, always, always either begun with or finished with:

In the Name of Jesus

If for some reason you are unable to cast out the spirit...I bind you (to tie up, exercise legal authority).

I rebuke you. (In Jesus' Name), or, the Lord rebuke you.   JUDE 9

I break your power.

I cancel your assignment.

Come out in Jesus' Name.

Be quiet!

Remove yourself from this (person), body, mind, soul and spirit. You will not hurt them.

The Blood of Jesus is against you.

Go! In Jesus' Name—to the dry places, to the dry uninhabited places!

I come against you in the Name of Jesus.

In the Name of Jesus Christ of Nazareth, I command you, spirit of _____, to loose (call their name) and let him/her go, NOW!

Pray positively over the person infilling in them the opposite of what you have cast out.

Rededicate that one to purity and holiness.

Pray the opposite of every problem the person had.

Pray a blessing over the person.

The person should receive a blessing from you and be infilled by you with the fruits of the Spirit.

CHAPTER 13

****

CASTING OUT DEVILS

****

WARNING: Casting out devils is not for everyone. This is not a game or to be entered into lightly. You must be born again and Spirit filled. You must not have any fear of the demonic or of dying. You must know who you are in Christ and be confident of your authority in Christ. If you are not completely right with God, you can get beat up physically by the demons you're trying to cast out. I really believe you must be called to do this. If you're not sure, then don't attempt it!

The person being ministered to needs to be silent while being ministered to. Tell them to remain silent, eyes open and watch to see what God's going to do for them. You can't receive into your spirit if you're speaking out at the same time. Afterwards, have them say "Thank you Jesus".

C.H. Spurgeon said "The Word of God is like a lion. You don't have to defend it, just open the cage door."

Psalm 3:8: "From the Lord comes deliverance. May your blessing be on Your people."
2 Corinthians 3:17 Where Jesus is Lord, there is freedom.

DICTIONARY

DEMON: a devil or evil spirit, energetic, forceful.

SPIRIT: A disembodied soul, not associated with a body.

REBUKE: To reprove sharply or severely.

REPROOF: An expression of condemnation for a fault or offense.

How did Jesus deal with demons?

1. Jesus called entities demons and evil spirits.
Matthew 12:28; Luke 11:24

2. Jesus spoke to the demons.
Mark 8:31-32; Mark 9:25

3. Demons spoke to Jesus.   Luke 4:41
   a) Sickness doesn't talk.
   b) They spoke in complete sentences.

    c)   They know who Jesus is.

    d)   They begged for mercy.

4.   No demon can ever be victorious over Jesus.
                                Romans 8:38-39

5.   Some people will turn away from God and follow demonic spirits and demonic teaching.   1 Timothy 4:1

6.   People brought the demon possessed to Jesus and He healed them.
                Matthew 4:24; Matthew 8:16

7.   Jesus laid hands on people, one at a time.
                                    Luke 4:40

8.   Jesus rebuked the demons and told them to be quiet.   Luke 4:35, 41

9.   Demons can cry out, shriek, with a loud, deep, terrible cry.   Luke 4:33; Mark 5:7

10. Demons have knowledge of things which are unknown to human beings.
                    Luke 4:34; Mark 5:6

11. Jesus told the demon to come out of the person.   Luke 4:35;

12. He drove them out with one word.
                              Matthew 8:16

13. The demon threw the person on the ground and then it came out without injuring the man.   Luke 4:35

14. People were amazed. Jesus spoke to the demon with authority and power.

Characteristics of a demon possessed man
As found in Luke 8 and Mark 5

Luke 8:27:   He wore no clothes.

Luke 8:28:   He was homeless

Mark 5:5:   He would cry out and cut himself.

Luke 8:29; Mark 5:4   The demon within him had superhuman strength.

Luke 8:29:   The person had been driven into isolation by the demon.

Luke 8:28; Mark 5:7, 10:   When the demon inside the person saw Jesus, it fell at Jesus' feet, shouting and begging for mercy.

Luke 8:31; Mark 5:10:	The demons begged not to be sent into the deep, the bottomless abyss.
Luke 8:35; Mark 5:15:	After the evils spirits came out of the man, he sat quietly, dressed, in his right mind.
Luke 8:39; Mark 5:19-20:	Jesus told the man to tell people of God's mercy and what He had done for him.

Demons can speak more than one language. The person to whom you are MINISTERING may need an interpreter, but the demon KNOWS ENGLISH very well, including profanity and obscenities. The problem that can occur, if you use an interpreter to tell the demon to get out, is that the interpreter may know not their position and authority in Christ like you do, and the demon may refuse to leave. The demon doesn't understand tongues. Don't speak in tongues during this time.

Unbelievers can be delivered from demonic problems. However, it is best if they receive Jesus Christ as Savior before any deliverance is scheduled. They must be willing and want to receive deliverance.

YOUR CREDENTIALS FOR CASTING OUT DEVILS

1. You must be a believer.   Mark 16:17

2. If you are in Christ, all things are under your feet.   Ephesians 1:21-23

3. You have power in Jesus Christ.
   Matthew 16:18; 2 Corinthians 10:4.

4. You have divine protection in Jesus Christ.
   Luke 10:14

   a) The Word of God. It's your protective armor.

   b) The Blood of Jesus. It has Divine power over all.

   c) The authority of the believer. Jesus said we will cast out devils.   Mark 16:17

   d) The Holy Spirit said He will lead us into all truth.   John 16:13

   e) The gifts of the Spirit.
   1 Corinthians 12. Truth destroys fear and error.

You cannot go into demonic territory without the authority and leadership of Jesus.

I feel, in my spirit, that verbal demons should be forbidden to speak. They should be ordered to be silent in Jesus' Name. Demons lie, but there are times they will speak truth. It doesn't matter what their name is. Don't hold a conversation with them. Demons cannot just attack people at their will. They must have legal grounds or an open door to be able to enter into someone. If a demon refuses to come out, the area (the authority) by which they are there to begin with, may still be there. Demons may come in through a person's nose or mouth or any other bodily opening. They will exit the same way they came in: i.e. tears, a cough, sneezing, burping, throwing up, sighing, urinating, flatulence. Tears may flow from the person. They may exit screaming.

> Demons have emotions. They believe, and tremble.   James 2:19

We must be careful whom we allow to lay hands on us and pray, because spirits can transfer through the hands. Before ministering, be sure to cover your body and soul with the Blood of Jesus.

Demons are the enemy, and there are symptoms of their activity: Persistent, recurrent, evil, destructive emotions, attitudes or behaviors.

Demons manifest in compulsive, out of control behavior, exploding outside or closing people up inside, shutting everyone out. Demons show themselves by unnatural attraction to occult things. Many times people, even Christian people who love the

Lord, don't even know they're being demonically oppressed.

A team for deliverance is very effective — silent prayer and silent casting out is strengthening for whomever is taking the lead. There should be a Pastoral covering and blessing and approval for this ministry. In other words, you need to be an active member of a church. Your Pastor must be familiar with you and approve of your ministry and "send you out" with prayer, protection and blessing.

DETECTING DEMONIC PRESENCE

Sin, thoughts, addictions. The person doesn't want it this way. Family histories of these ungodly things.

Helplessness – over emotions, a condition or situation. The person can't seem to get victory over it. There's just something there they can't "put their finger on". They just want to be completely clean.

Something extremely negative, i.e. anger, rage comes over them.

A voice told me to kill myself. This may be a spirit of death or suicide. There could be a multiple personality of suicide here.

Past involvement or family involvement in: Witchcraft, satansim. Freemasonry or addictions.

Possible demonic entry areas:

A victim of: Child molestation, incest/rape, hereditary rage, hereditary negative behavior, deliberate sin, pornography, adultery, abortion, occult, séance, ouija board, horoscope, fortune telling, bitterness, unforgiveness, addictions such as alcohol, nicotine, sex, gambling, food, shopping; compulsive exercising; homosexuality, promiscuity, rejection by parents, spouse, boyfriends, friends, teachers, church. The list is endless.

Rejected parents produce rejected children. Anxiety, worry, depression, mental illness, suicide, mental problems, family history of chronic sickness: heart, diabetes, allergies, accidents, early death, brain damage, anger, rage, temper, violence, pride, anti social behavior.

Deliverance can even be administered by proxy, with someone spiritually and emotionally close to those under oppression. Distance is unimportant.

Jesus did it without the person being there. There's no distance with God.

Actual deliverance session

Deliverance should be administered by a male to a male, a female to a female. If a man prays for a woman, another woman or other man should be present. A team of at least 2 or 3 people ministering is ideal. Only the main ministry person should out loud speak at a time. The others should pray or agree in the casting out in silence. If a team member has discernment from the Lord, this should be written on paper and passed discretely on to the person leading. Paper tissues, water, anointing oil and lined trash container should be on hand.

Before the participant arrives pray for and cover yourselves and the participant, for family, home, pets and vehicles with the Blood of Jesus and against any transference of spirits.

The room should be prepared by anointing it with oil, casting out anything that could be in there and low worship music played. The team members should pray for one another before the participant arrives.

People should be prayed for in private and the information they have given you is strictly confidential within the team and your leader. The only one the information may be shared with is your department head, should the information be of such a serious legal nature.

Fasting beforehand by the ministry team and the participant may open up understanding. It's important to remember to stay humble, that the team is really nothing. God is doing the deliverance. You're only the donkey whom He is using at this time. It's not that long ago that you were in the same condition as the participant. Isaiah 58:6-7: Jesus spoke to His disciples about how some demons only come out by prayer and fasting. Matthew 17:21; Mark 9:29. In 1 Corinthians 7:5, we're told to give ourselves to fasting and prayer. The fasting does not have to be food if you're not able. God can lead you to make some kind of a sacrifice for the purpose of this deliverance.

The person must be saved, willing, and desire deliverance. They should never be forced. Have them repeat a prayer similar to this before you begin:

I confess Jesus Christ to be my personal Savior. I confess, renounce and reject every sin that I, my parents or my ancestors may have committed and which has brought anything negative upon my life. I ask for forgiveness for myself and for them. I turn away from any behavior that is not pleasing to you Oh God. I renounce the devil and all his works and influences in my life. I claim release from all demonic influence in my life. I claim freedom in Jesus' Name! He is Lord of my whole life and I want no other in control of me but Him. In Jesus' Name. Amen.

The participant who wishes deliverance should be seated in a straight backed chair away from any other furniture other than the chairs of the ministry team. They should be facing the chair of the one who will be the main ministry person. The other ministry team person's chairs should be to the side of the participant.

Demons must never be permitted to take control. The demons should be instructed at the very beginning of the session that when called out they are to obey and come out and go where instructed. They are not to harm the participant or anyone else ministering.

The participant should be told that they have their will over the demons and it may be necessary for them to verbally agree to the removal of the demons, that you will be speaking to any demons and not to them personally. They are to agree silently in their minds at all other times.

A demon may show their anger towards anyone operating beyond their faith level or spiritual condition. The team must always strive to personal holiness in their own life and maintain as close a walk as possible with our God. Church attendance, Bible study, personal Bible study, prayer and devotion to God at all times are a requirement for anyone on the deliverance team.

Be confident in your authority in Christ, and in your use of the Name of Jesus.

The participant being ministered to is to be instructed to keep silent at all times during the ministry, unless they feel they need to share something pertinent to what is being dealt with at that time, or if they experience any unusual symptoms or pain during the session. They are to bring this to the attention of the team. This could be a demonic manifestation that needs to be anointed with oil and immediately dealt with by the team. The voice that may come from them may not be theirs, i.e. a woman speaking in a man's voice, a man speaking in a woman's voice, an adult speaking like a child. There may be harsh words spoken at you or the demon may scream in your face. Just tell it to be quiet, in Jesus' Name.

Demons can cause people to act out of character: superhuman strength, violent and obscene behavior, tantrums, kicking, biting, yelling, screaming, scratching, and clenched fists in anger. Don't resist the clenched fist or be threatened by it. Instead of giving into human response by tightening your grip on their hands, release your grip on them. The opposite works on the demons. Remember the Greater Power is within you.

Deliverance is not based on feelings. Never ask the participant how they feel after the session ends.

The question focuses on feelings rather than faith. The evidence of deliverance will be apparent to you by the person's face. Assure them that God has done a great work in them, that they are free! If the participant indicates they don't feel any different, tell them that it's not necessary that they feel something. By faith, we know it's been done, that they are free! It still happened. There may be no evident sign that bondages have been broken. Your participant may be very quiet and seemingly non responsive to your casting out. Don't worry about it. They're leaving anyway.

The participants need to be encouraged to attend the final deliverance session which will enable them to remain free. They may still need your encouragement after the deliverance is completed. Love them. Hug them.

ALL PRAYER IN PUBLIC SHOULD BE DONE WITH OPEN EYES. "Watch and pray", Jesus said.

As indicated earlier, there are many signs of demons exiting your participant. Here again, is probably a partial list: coughing, sighing, yawning, belching, gagging, vomiting, sneezing, throat clearing, spitting. Signs of manifestation may include but not be limited to: growling or moaning, watering or teary eyes, slight movement of the head, the whites of their eyes becoming black, movement of the head indicating "no", refusal to come out. You just tell them something like: "You're defeated in Jesus' Name. You come out now in the Name of Jesus."

Remain relaxed and nonchalant when dealing with demons. Maintain an air of quietness, even if you're given startling information.

After the prayer of deliverance all remaining demons should be ordered out in Jesus' Name.

If there are multiple demons, you can cast them out all at one time. Jesus didn't name the demons when He cast out "Legion".

Pride is a good place to start with your participant.

They may not really believe they have anything demonic within themselves. Rejection is another one all of us seem to have.

If a person refuses to cooperate, it is obviously not God's time for them to be delivered.

If the person tries to cough and is unable to do so, but may only be able to clear their throat, this may be caused by strong spirits of resistance. Authority should be taken strongly over every spirit of anti Christ, rebellion, resistance, and spiritual darkness.

If the person feels like they're choking, anoint their throat with oil and speak the manifestation away in Jesus' Name.

When there is laughter from the participant, this is probably a spirit of mockery and it may be pride as well.

TIPS FOR THE DELIVERANCE TEAM

<u>BE PERSISTENT</u> Demons will try to bluff you, pretend they're gone when they're not.

REASSURE the participant that you're not talking to them personally, but to any demon that may be present inside of them.

Demonic noise and speech should not be permitted.

Quiet it, in Jesus' Name.

When you feel all demons are out, check again.

Command all demonic powers which remain to come out. If you feel that for some reason they won't come out, then bind them so they can never again manifest or torment the participant.

AFTER THE DEMONS LEAVE

Bless the participant and infill them with the opposite of what has come out of them. Luke 11:25

When demons are bound in the Name of Jesus, they no longer have the power to bind or dominate people. Mark 6:7; Mark 7:29; Mark 12:29; Mark 16:17; Luke 10:17

Sometimes spirits that have been bound and ordered to leave have not done so because the persons in whom they were living did not strongly want them to leave or the person has unbelief.

PEOPLE ON WHOM DELIVERANCE SHOULD NOT BE ATTEMPTED:

Anyone who is unwilling to cooperate and release the negative things in their life.

Those receiving medical or psychiatric care for mental problems.

Those who refuse to believe that their problems are from demonic causes.

Those who do not believe Jesus can free them.

Christians who are against deliverance.

Deliverance team members must be spiritually right with God and free from all forms of satanic oppression.

Jesus Christ must be honored above all. The glory all belongs to Him.

Deliverance sessions are not times for counseling.

You may or may not want to use the word "demon" with children. Although, today with the television and all it's demonic programming, it depends upon the child. You can refer to demons as evil powers. I remember years ago, as a brand new Christian, I dressed up one Halloween as a vampire green lipstick, long dress, long wig, complete with vampire teeth, and we put appropriate music into the yard. I was going to have fun giving out candy to the children that would come. One child came and was so educated with vampires and they suggested I hold my mouth open a little more so my teeth could show better. Another child came to the door and was so frightened that they backed up off the stoop and fell down. In my natural reaction, I stepped forward to help them and the child shrank back from me in terror. After that, I changed my clothes and got dressed normally again. God forgave me for my ignorance.

IN ORDER TO STAY FREE:

Freely love God and other people, without conditions.

Read the Word of God daily. Joshua 1:8; Psalm 119:9-11; 2 Timothy 2:15.

Be a disciple of Jesus Christ. Tell others about what God has done for you through Jesus.

Live a moral and ethical life that no one can question.

Decide each day to make good choices. "what would Jesus do?" Ephesians 4:22-23, 27; Romans 8:12-17

Pray. Keep an attitude of gratitude.

The devil is a liar! John 8:44. Be on guard for his deceptions. James 4:1-8; 1 Corinthians 10:13; 2 Peter 2:9

Jesus has freed you from condemnation. Romans 8:1; John 8:36.

Don't play with deliberate sin. Confess sin immediately and don't repeat it. Leviticus 11:44-45; 1 Peter 1:16

Ask the Holy Spirit to help you make Jesus Lord over you completely, body, soul and spirit. Romans 12:2-8; Ephesians 5:18

Put on the protective armor of God each day. Joshua 17:5; Matthew 6:13; Ephesians 6:10-18; Hebrews 2:17-18.

You're never alone. God is always with you. Hebrews 13:5-6; Deuteronomy 31:6; Psalm 118:6-7; Matthew 28:20.

Cut yourself off from the wrong people. Choose Christ honoring friends. James 4:4.

Set yourself free again after initial deliverance has taken place, if need be, in the Name of Jesus: Refuse in Jesus' Name to go back where you were. Cast them out of yourself in Jesus' Name. Ask God to completely fill you with Himself. "I take authority over you demon spirits in the Name of Jesus Christ. I command you to leave me NOW in Jesus' Name and go to the dry and uninhabited places in Jesus' Name."

TO SUMMARIZE

Name the spirit.

Order it out in Jesus' Name.

Command it to go to dry and uninhabited places and not to return.

Pray a blessing on the participant

Infill the participant with the opposite of what you have cast out.

Don't get discouraged if things don't happen the first time you command it. Remember: Elijah laid himself on the dead child three times. Elijah prayed seven times for rain before it came. Jesus prayed three times in the Garden of Gethsemane.

SUGGESTED READING/ RESOURCES USED

ALL TOPICS
THE WORD OF GOD

AUTHORITY & POWER:
<u>Benny Hinn</u> "The Anointing"

FAITH:
<u>Kenneth Hagin</u>   "Words"

<u>Bill Johnson</u>   "When Heaven Invades Earth"

<u>Oral Roberts</u>   "How Your Faith Works When God Says NO!", "How To Find Your Point of Contact"

GOD:
<u>Pat Robertson</u>   "NAMES OF GOD"

HEALING:
Charles & Frances Hunter   "How to Heal the Sick"
    "Handbook for Healing" "Healing School"

Joy Dawson   "Some of the Ways of God in Healing"

Andrew Murray   "Divine Healing"

HEALING:
R. W. Shambach   "God's Guarantee to Heal You"

Bishop Paul Crites   TAPE MESSAGE: "Covenant of Healing"

Kenneth Hagin   "God's Word, A Never Failing Remedy", "The Healing Anointing", "Forgiveness and The Blood".

T. F. Tenney   "Secret Sources of Power"

F. F. Bosworth   "Christ the Healer"

Benny Hinn   "The Blood"

Oral Roberts   "If You Need Healing, Do These Things", "What to Do When Your Healing Seems Slow in Coming"

Richard Roberts   "How to Know God Wants to Heal You"

DELIVERANCE
Noel & Phyl Gibson "Evicting Demonic Intruders", "Freedom in Christ"

DELIVERANCE
Neil T. Anderson   "The Bondage Breaker"

John Eckhardt   "Identifying and Breaking Curses"

Win Worley   "Demolishing the Hosts of Hell", "Eradicating the Hosts of Hell: "Annihilating the Hosts of Hell".

Oral Roberts   "How to Resist the Devil and his demons"

Mark I. Bubeck   "Spiritual Warfare Prayers"

Ron Phillips   "Vanquishing the Enemy"

PRAISE, WORSHIP
Robert Gay   "Silencing the Enemy"

Dr. Myles Munroe   "The Purpose & Power of Praise & Worship".

Gloria Copeland   "Build Yourself An Ark"

TITHES & OFFERINGS
Oral Roberts   "Seed Faith 2000"

Juanita Bynam   "The Planted Seed"

WARFARE
Carol Rucci   "Fight the Good Fight of Faith"

C. Peter Wagner   "Warfare Prayer"

Mark I. Bubeck   "Spiritual Warfare Prayers"

WORDS
Kenneth Hagin   "In Him"

devil
C. S. Lovett   "Dealing with the Devil"

Ron Phillips   "Vanquishing the Enemy"

Kenneth E. Hagin   "The Believer's Authority".

Kenneth Hagin   "The Triumphant Church; God's Word, A Never Failing Remedy".

HINTS TO WIN THE BATTLE OVER ALL SICKNESS AND DISEASE

(unknown author)

THE WORD OF GOD WILL SAVE YOUR LIFE   PROVERBS 4:20-23

GOD'S WORD WILL NOT FAIL
                    JOSHUA 21:45

GOD IS WILLING TO HEAL YOU FOR HIS GOOD PLEASURE
                    PHILIPPIANS 2:13

THE SPIRIT OF LIFE IS MAKING YOUR BODY ALIVE.

                    ROMANS 8:11

GOD IS FOR YOU.
                          2 CORINTHIANS 1:20

IT IS GOD'S WILL FOR YOU TO BE
HEALED.   MATTHEW 8:2-3

OBEY GOD'S WORD AND BE HEALED.
                          EXODUS 15:26

SERVE THE LORD AND HEALING WILL
BE YOURS.   EXODUS 23:25

GOD TAKES ALL SICKNESS AWAY
FROM YOU.   DEUTERONOMY 7:15

OBEY ALL GOD'S COMMANDMENTS
AND RECEIVE ALL GOD'S BLESSINGS.
                          MALACHI 3:10

ONE OF GOD'S BENEFITS IS HEALING.
                          PSALM 103:1-5

GOD'S WORD IS HEALING.
                          PSALM 107:20

GOD WANTS YOU TO LIVE.
                          PSALM 118:17

CHOOSE TO LIVE. BE A FIGHTER!
                          DEUTERONOMY 30:19

YOU WILL LIVE A LONG LIFE.

PSALM 91:16

WITH THE STRIPES THAT WOUNDED
JESUS, WE ARE HEALED.

ISAIAH 53:5

GOD WILL RESTORE YOUR HEALTH

JEREMIAH 30:17

YOU CAN TAKE AUTHORITY OVER
THE SICKNESS IN YOUR BODY.

MATTHEW 18:18

AGREE WITH OTHER BELIEVERS FOR
YOUR HEALING.   MATTHEW 18:19

WHAT YOU SAY WILL MAKE A
DIFFERENCE.   MARK 11:22-23

BELIEVE, AND YOU WILL RECEIVE.

MARK 11:24

PLEAD YOUR CASE TO GOD.

ISAIAH 43:25-26

HAVE A SPIRIT-FILLED BELIEVER LAY
HANDS ON YOU FOR HEALING.

MARK 16:17-18

WORSHIP GOD AND HE WILL LISTEN.

JOHN 9:31

THE DEVIL WANTS TO KILL YOU; GOD WANTS TO HEAL YOU.   JOHN 10:10

YOU ARE REDEEMED FROM THE CURSE.   GALATIANS 3:13-14

YOU SHALL NOT WAIVER IN YOUR FAITH.   HEBREWS 10:23

YOU CAN HAVE CONFIDENCE IN GOD AND HIS WORD.   HEBREWS 10:35

YOU CAN FIND STRENGTH IN GOD AND IN HIS WORD   JOEL 3:10

JESUS CHRIST HAS NEVER CHANGED. WHAT HE DID IN THE BIBLE, HE WILL DO FOR YOU TODAY.
              HEBREWS 13:8

GOD'S HIGHEST WISH IS FOR YOU TO BE WELL.   3 JOHN 2

BE ANOINTED WITH OIL BY A CHRISTIAN WHO BELIEVES IN HEALING.   JAMES 5:14-15

JESUS HAS ALREADY PAID THE PRICE FOR YOUR HEALING.   1 PETER 2:24

BE CONFIDENT IN YOUR PRAYERS.
              1 JOHN 5:13-15

GODANSWERSTHEPRAYERSOFTHOSE
WHO KEEP HIS COMMANDMENTS.
1 JOHN 3:21-22

FEAR IS NOT OF GOD. REBUKE IT!
2 TIMOTHY 1:7

CAST DOWN THOSE THOUGHTS AND
IMAGINATIONS THAT DON'T LINE UP
WITH THE WORD OF GOD.
2 CORINTHIANS 10:4-5

BE STRONG IN THE LORD'S POWER.
PUT ON HIS ARMOR TO FIGHT FOR
YOUR HEALING.   EPHESIANS 6:10-13

GIVE TESTIMONY OF YOUR HEALING
WHEN IT COMES.   REVELATION 12:11

HEALING SCRIPTURES

NEW KING JAMES VERSION

"Praying the actual scriptures is one of the most powerful things you can ever learn in life." John Bevere.

I WORSHIP YOU LORD GOD OF HEAVEN; I WORSHIP YOU FOR YOUR PROMISES. JESUS, YOU BORE MY SICKNESSES. I WILL NOT BEAR IT. THANK YOU BECAUSE YOUR WORD SAYS BY YOUR STRIPES I AM HEALED. MY GOD, IN THE NAME OF JESUS CHRIST THE WORD WILL WORK FOR ME. LORD, IF I HAVE ANY SIN BEFORE ME, I'M SORRY. FORGIVE ME, IN JESUS' NAME.

EXODUS 15:11 WHO IS LIKE YOU O LORD, AMONG THE GODS? WHO IS LIKE YOU, GLORIOUS IN HOLINESS, FEARFUL IN PRAISES, DO WONDERS?

PSALM 9:9&10 THE LORD ALSO WILL BE A REFUGE FOR THE OPPRESSED, A REFUGE IN TIMES OF TROUBLE. AND THEY THAT KNOW YOUR NAME WILL TRUST IN YOU, FOR YOU LORD HAVE NOT FORSAKEN THEM THAT SEEK YOU.

EXODUS 15:6 YOUR RIGHT HAND, O LORD, IS BECOME GLORIOUS IN POWER; YOUR RIGHT HAND O LORD HAS DASHED IN PIECES THE ENEMY.

EPHESIANS 2:6 AND (GOD) HAS RAISED US UP TOGETHER IN HEAVENLY PLACES IN CHRIST JESUS.

PSALM 5:12 FOR YOU, LORD, WILL BLESS THE RIGHTEOUS WITH FAVOR; YOU WILL COMPASS HIM AS WITH A SHIELD.

PSALM 18:1-3, 30 I LOVE YOU, O LORD, MY STRENGTH. THE LORD IS MY ROCK AND MY FORTRESS AND MY DELIVERER, MY GOD, MY STRENGTH, IN WHOM I WILL TRUST; MY BUCKLER AND THE HORN OF MY SALVATION AND MY HIGH TOWER. I WILL CALL UPON THE LORD, WHO IS WORTHY TO BE PRAISED. SO SHALL I BE SAVED FROM MY ENEMIES. AS FOR GOD, HIS WAY IS PERFECT; THE WORD OF THE LORD TRIED; HE IS A BUCKLER TO ALL THOSE THAT TRUST IN HIM.

PSALM 29:11 THE LORD WILL GIVE STRENGTH TO HIS PEOPLE. THE LORD WILL BLESS HIS PEOPLE WITH PEACE.

ISAIAH 26:3-4, 12 YOU SHALL KEEP HIM IN PERFECT PEACE, WHOSE MIND IS STAYED ON YOU, BECAUSE HE TRUSTS IN YOU. TRUST IN THE LORD FOREVER, FOR IN THE LORD JEHOVAH IS EVERLASTING STRENGTH. LORD YOU WILL ESTABLISH PEACE FOR US, FOR YOU ALSO HAVE DONE ALL OUR WORKS IN US.

GENESIS 18:25 SHALL NOT THE JUDGE OF ALL EARTH DO RIGHT? (YES, HE WILL!!!!)

ISAIAH 55:11 SO SHALL MY WORD BE THAT GOES FORTH FROM MY MOUTH; IT SHALL NOT RETURN TO ME VOID. BUT, IT SHALL ACCOMPLISH WHAT I PLEASE, AND IT SHALL PROSPER IN THE THING FOR WHICH I SENT IT.

GALATIANS 3:13-14 CHRIST HAS REDEEMED US FROM THE CURSE OF THE LAW, BEING MADE A CURSE FOR US; FOR IT IS WRITTEN, CURSED IS EVERY ONE THAT HANGS ON A TREE; THAT THE BLESSING OF ABRAHAM MIGHT COME ON THE GENTILES THROUGH JESUS CHRIST; THAT WE MIGHT RECEIVE THE PROMISE OF THE SPIRIT THROUGH FAITH.

<u>PROVERBS 10:24</u> BUT THE DESIRE OF THE RIGHTEOUS SHALL BE GRANTED.

<u>PROVERBS 4:20-22</u> MY SON, ATTEND TO MY WORDS; INCLINE YOUR EAR TO MY SAYINGS. LET THEM NOT DEPART FROM YOUR EYES; KEEP THEM IN THE MIDST OF YOUR HEART. FOR THEY ARE LIFE TO THOSE THAT FIND THEM, AND HEALTH TO ALL THEIR FLESH.

<u>LUKE 10:19</u> BEHOLD I GIVE YOU THE AUTHORITY TO TRAMPLE ON SERPENTS AND SCORPIONS, AND OVER ALL THE POWER OF THE ENEMY, AND NOTHING SHALL BY ANY MEANS HURT YOU.

<u>PSALM 34:15, 17 & 19</u> THE EYES OF THE LORD ARE UPON THE RIGHTEOUS; HIS EARS ARE OPEN TO THEIR CRY. THE RIGHTEOUS CRY AND THE LORD HEARS AND DELIVERS THEM OUT OF THEIR TROUBLES. MANY ARE THE AFFLICTIONS OF THE RIGHTEOUS, BUT THE LORD DELIVERED THEM OUT OF THEM ALL.

<u>PSALM 32:7</u> YOU ARE MY HIDING PLACE. YOU SHALL PRESERVE ME FROM TROUBLE; YOU SHALL SURROUND ME WITH SONGS OF DELIVERANCE.

<u>GENESIS 15:1</u> FEAR NOT, I AM YOUR SHIELD AND GREAT EXCEEDING GREAT REWARD.

PSALM 138:2 & 7 I WILL PRAISE YOUR NAME FOR YOUR LOVING KINDNESS AND FOR YOUR TRUTH; FOR YOU HAVE MAGNIFIED YOUR WORD ABOVE YOUR NAME. THOUGH I WALK IN THE MIDST OF TROUBLE, YOU WILL REVIVE ME; YOU SHALL STRETCH FORTH YOUR HAND AGAINST THE WRATH OF MY ENEMIES, AND YOUR RIGHT HAND SHALL SAVE ME.

PSALM 129:4 THE LORD IS RIGHTEOUS; HE HAS CUT ASUNDER THE CORDS OF THE WICKED.

PSALM 17:4 BY THE WORD OF MY LIPS I HAVE KEPT ME FROM THE PATHS OF THE DESTROYER.

FATHER I THANK YOU FOR YOUR WORD, THAT YOUR WORD WILL NOT RETURN TO YOU VOID. FATHER, I THANK YOU THAT YOUR WORD IS TRUE AND ANOINTED.

COLOSSIANS 2:10, 15 AND YOU ARE COMPLETE IN HIM (JESUS) WHICH IS HEAD OF ALL PRINCIPALITY AND POWER. (JESUS), HAVING SPOILED PRINCIPALITIES AND POWERS, HE MADE A SHOW OF THEM OPENLY, TRIUMPHING OVER THEM IN IT.

1 PETER 3:22 JESUS WHO GONE INTO HEAVEN, AND IS ON THE RIGHT HAND OF

GOD, ANGELS AND AUTHORITIES AND POWERS BEING MADE SUBJECT UNTO HIM.

2 CORINTHIANS 4:7 BUT WE HAVE THIS TREASURE IN EARTHEN VESSELS, THAT THE EXCELLENCY OF THE POWER MAY BE OF GOD AND NOT US.

DEUTERONOMY 26:15 LOOK DOWN FROM YOUR HOLY HABITATION, FROM HEAVEN, AND BLESS YOUR PEOPLE.

DEUTERONOMY 26:10 I HAVE BROUGHT THE FIRST FRUITS OF THE LAND, WHICH YOU, O LORD HAS GIVEN ME AND JESUS THE GREAT HIGH PRIEST HAS SET IT BEFORE THE LORD YOUR GOD, AND SHALL WORSHIP BEFORE THE LORD YOUR GOD.

PSALM 9:10 AND THEY THAT KNOW YOUR NAME WILL TRUST IN YOU, FOR YOU LORD HAVE NOT FORSAKEN THEM THAT SEEK YOU.

EPHESIANS 5:2 CHRIST HAS GIVEN HIMSELF FOR US AN OFFERING AND A SACRIFICE TO GOD FOR A SWEET SMELLING SAVOR.

THANK YOU HOLY SPIRIT FOR YOUR ANOINTING AS I SPEAK GOD'S WORDS GRACIOUSLY AND HUMBLY.

ROMANS 8:2, 37 FOR THE LAW OF THE SPIRIT OF LIFE IN CHRIST JESUS HAS MADE ME FREE FROM THE LAW OF SIN AND DEATH. IN ALL THESE THINGS WE ARE MORE THAN CONQUERORS THROUGH HIM THAT LOVED US.

1 JOHN 4:4 YOU ARE OF GOD LITTLE CHILDREN, AND HAVE OVERCOME THEM, BECAUSE GREATER IS HE THAT IS IN ME THAT HE THAT IS IN THE WORLD.

REVELATION 1:17 FEAR NOT, I AM THE FIRST AND THE LAST; I AM HE THAT LIVES AND WAS DEAD, AND BEHOLD I AM ALIVE FOREVERMORE, AMEN; AND HAVE THE KEYS TO HELL AND OF DEATH.

DEUTERONOMY 8:18 BUT YOU SHALL REMEMBER THE LORD YOUR GOD, FOR IT IS HE THAT GIVES YOU POWER TO GET WEALTH (HEALTH).

JOHN 8:32 AND YOU SHALL KNOW THE TRUTH AND THE TRUTH SHALL MAKE YOU FREE.

JOHN 6:63 IT IS THE SPIRIT THAT QUICKENS, THE FLESH PROFITS NOTHING; THE WORDS THAT I SPEAK UNTO YOU, THEY ARE SPIRIT, AND THEY ARE LIFE.

<u>PROVERBS 8:35</u> FOR WHO FINDS ME FINDS LIFE AND SHALL OBTAIN FAVOR OF THE LORD.

<u>PSALM 36:9</u> FOR WITH YOU IS THE FOUNTAIN OF LIFE.

<u>JEREMIAH 30:17</u> FOR I WILL RESTORE HEALTH UNTO YOU, AND I WILL HEAL YOU OF YOUR WOUNDS, SAYS THE LORD.

<u>DEUTERONOMY 28:1-14</u> BLESSED SHALL BE THE FRUIT OF YOUR BODY...BLESSED SHALL YOU BE WHEN YOU COME IN. BLESSED SHALL YOU BE WHEN YOU GO OUT. THE LORD SHALL CAUSE YOUR ENEMIES THAT RISE UP AGAINST YOU TO BE SMITTEN BEFORE MY FACE; THEY SHALL COME OUT AGAINST YOU ONE WAY AND GOD WILL CAUSE THEM TO FLEE BEFORE YOU SEVEN WAYS. (PRAISE GOD!) THE LORD SHALL MAKE YOU PLENTEOUS IN GOODS, IN THE FRUIT OF YOUR BODY; AND THE LORD SHALL MAKE YOU THE HEAD AND NOT THE TAIL; AND I SHALL BE ABOVE ONLY, AND SHALL NOT BE BENEATH.

<u>JOHN 14:27</u> PEACE I LEAVE WITH YOU. MY PEACE I GIVE YOU, NOT AS THE WORLD GIVES DO I GIVE TO YOU; LET NOT YOUR HEART BE TROUBLED, NEITHER LET IT BE AFRAID.

HEBREWS 4: 12 FOR THE WORD OF GOD IS QUICK AND POWERFUL AND SHARPER THAN ANY TWO-EDGED SWORD, PIERCING EVEN TO THE DIVIDING ASUNDER OF SOUL AND SPIRIT, AND OF THE JOINTS AND MARROW, AND IS A DISCERNER OF THE THOUGHTS AND INTENTS OF THE HEART.

EXODUS 15:26 I AM THE LORD THAT HEALS YOU.

EXODUS 23:25 AND YOU SHALL SERVE THE LORD YOUR GOD, AND HE SHALL BLESS YOUR BREAD AND YOUR WATER. I WILL TAKE SICKNESS AWAY FROM THE MIDST OF YOU.

DEUTERONOMY 7:15 THE LORD WILL TAKE AWAY FROM YOU ALL SICKNESS. YOU SHALL BE BLESSED ABOVE ALL PEOPLE.

JOSHUA 21:45 THERE FAILED NOT ANYTHING OF ANY GOOD THING WHICH THE LORD HAD SPOKEN TO THE HOUSE OF ISRAEL; ALL CAME TO PASS.

PSALM 103:1-5 BLESS THE LORD, O MY SOUL, AND ALL THAT IS WITHIN ME, BLESS HIS HOLY NAME. BLESS THE LORD, O MY SOUL, AND FORGET NOT ALL HIS BENEFITS; WHO FORGIVES ALL MY INIQUITIES; WHO HEALS ALL MY DISEASES; WHO REDEEMED MY

LIFE FROM DESTRUCTION; WHO CROWNED ME WITH LOVING KINDNESS AND TENDER MERCIES; WHO SATISFIES MY MOUTH WITH GOOD THINGS SO THAT MY YOUTH IS RENEWED LIKE THE EAGLES.

ISAIAH 53:4-5 SURELY HE HAS BORNE OUR GRIEFS, AND CARRIED OUR SORROWS, YET WE DID ESTEEM HIM STRICKEN, SMITTEN OF GOD AND AFFLICTED; BUT HE WAS WOUNDED FOR OUR TRANSGRESSION, HE WAS BRUISED FOR OUR INIQUITIES, THE CHASTISEMENT OF OUR PEACE WAS UPON HIM, AND WITH HIS STRIPES WE ARE HEALED.

JEREMIAH 32:27 BEHOLD I AM THE LORD, THE GOD OF ALL FLESH. IS THERE ANYTHING TOO HARD FOR ME? (NO THERE ISN'T!!!)

REVELATION 12:11 AND THEY OVERCAME HIM (THE devil) BY THE BLOOD OF THE LAMB AND BY THE WORD OF THEIR TESTIMONY.

PROVERBS 18:21 DEATH AND LIFE ARE IN THE POWER OF THE TONGUE AND THEY THAT LOVE IT SHALL EAT THE FRUIT THEREOF.

PSALM 139:14 I WILL PRAISE THEE, FOR I AM FEARFULLY AND WONDERFULLY MADE. MARVELOUS ARE YOUR WORKS AND MY SOUL KNOWS RIGHT WELL.

PSALM 30:5 EVERY WORD OF GOD IS PURE; HE IS A SHIELD TO THOSE WHO PUT THEIR TRUST IN HIM.

PSALM 107:20 (GOD) HE SENT HIS WORD, AND HEALED THEM.

2 CHRONICLES 32:8 BUT WITH US IS THE LORD OUR GOD TO HELP US AND TO FIGHT OUR BATTLES.

JEREMIAH 1:12 THEN SAID THE LORD TO ME, I WILL HASTEN MY WORD TO PERFORM IT.

NAHUM 1:9 WHAT DO YOU IMAGINE AGAINST THE LORD? HE WILL MAKE AN UTTER END; AFFLICTION SHALL NOT RISE UP THE SECOND TIME.

MALACHI 4:2 BUT TO YOU THAT FEAR MY NAME SHALL THE SON OF RIGHTEOUSNESS ARISE WITH HEALING IN HIS WINGS; AND YOU SHALL GO FORTH AND GROW UP AS CALVES OF THE STALL.

MATTHEW 8:17 THAT IT MIGHT BE FULFILLED WHICH WAS SPOKEN BY ISAIAH THE PROPHET, SAYING, HIMSELF TOOK OUR INFIRMITIES AND BORE OUR SICKNESSES.

MATTHEW 16: 18-19 THE GATES OF HELL SHALL NOT PREVAIL AGAINST GOD'S

CHURCH (ME!!!) AND I WILL GIVE YOU THE KEY OF THE KINGDOM OF HEAVEN AND WHATSOEVER THAT YOU SHALL BIND ON EARTH SHALL BE BOUND IN HEAVEN AND WHATSOEVER THOU SHALL LOOSE UPON EARTH SHALL BE LOOSED IN HEAVEN.

MATTHEW 17:20 IF YOU HAVE FAITH AS A GRAIN OF MUSTARD SEED, YOU SHALL SAY TO THIS MOUNTAIN, REMOVE (NOW) HENCE TO YONDER PLACE, AND IT SHALL REMOVE AND NOTHING SHALL BE IMPOSSIBLE TO YOU.

1 JOHN 3:18-22 MY LITTLE CHILDREN, LET US NOT LOVE IN WORD, NEITHER IN TONGUE, BUT IN DEED AND IN TRUTH; AND HEREBY WE KNOW THAT WE ARE OF THE TRUTH AND SHALL ASSURE OUR HEARTS BEFORE HIM, FOR IF OUR HEART CONDEMN US, GOD IS GREATER THAN OUR HEART, AND KNOWS ALL THINGS. BELOVED IF OUR HEART CONDEMN US NOT, THEN WE HAVE CONFIDENCE TOWARD GOD. AND WHAT SOEVER WE ASK, WE RECEIVE OF HIM BECAUSE WE KEEP HIS COMMANDMENTS, AND DO THOSE THINGS THAT ARE PLEASING IN HIS SIGHT.

ISAIAH 43:1-2 FEAR NOT, FOR I HAVE REDEEMED YOU. I HAVE CALLED YOU BY YOUR NAME; YOU ARE MINE. WHEN YOU

PASS THROUGH THE WATERS I WILL BE WITH YOU AND THROUGH THE RIVERS, THEY SHALL NOT OVERFLOW YOU; WHEN YOU WALK THROUGH THE FIRE, YOU SHALL NOT BE BURNED; NEITHER SHALL THE FLAME KINDLE UPON YOU, FOR I AM THE LORD YOUR GOD, THE HOLY ONE OF ISRAEL.

MARK 11:23-24 HAVE FAITH IN GOD. FOR TRULY I SAY TO YOU, THAT WHOSEVER SHALL SAY TO THIS MOUNTAIN, BE REMOVED AND CAST INTO THE SEA AND SHALL NOT DOUBT IN HIS HEART, BUT SHALL BELIEVE THAT THOSE THINGS WHICH HE SAID SHALL COME TO PASS; HE SHALL HAVE WHATSOEVER HE SAYS. THEREFORE I SAY TO YOU, WHAT THINGS SO EVER YOU DESIRE, WHEN YOU PRAY, BELIEVE THAT YOU RECEIVE THEM AND YOU SHALL HAVE THEM.

LUKE 3:5 PREPARE YOU THE WAY OF THE LORD, MAKE HIS PATH STRAIGHT; EVERY VALLEY SHALL BE FILLED AND EVERY MOUNTAIN AND HILL SHALL BE BROUGHT LOW AND THE CROOKED SHALL BE MADE STRAIGHT AND THE ROUGH WAYS SHALL BE MADE SMOOTH. (I CLAIM IT IN JESUS' NAME!!!)

MARK 16:17-18 AND THESE SIGNS SHALL FOLLOW THEM THAT BELIEVE; IN MY NAME

SHALL THEY CAST OUT DEVILS; THEY SHALL SPEAK WITH NEW TONGUES; THEY SHALL TAKE UP SERPENTS; AND IF THEY DRINK ANYTHING DEADLY, IT WILL NOT HURT THEM; THEY WILL LAY THEIR HANDS ON THE SICK, AND THEY WILL GET WELL.

JOHN 10:10 THE THIEF COMES BUT FOR TO STEAL AND TO KILL AND TO DESTROY; I'M COME THAT THEY MIGHT HAVE LIFE AND THAT THEY MIGHT HAVE IT MORE ABUNDANTLY.

EPHESIANS 1:3 BLESSED BE THE GOD AND FATHER OF OUR LORD JESUS CHRIST, WHO HAS BLESSED US WITH ALL SPIRITUAL BLESSINGS IN HEAVENLY PLACES IN CHRIST.

EPHESIANS 3:20 NOW TO HIM THAT IS ABLE TO DO EXCEEDINGLY ABUNDANTLY ABOVE ALL THAT WE ASK OR THINK, ACCORDING TO THE POWER THAT WORKS IN US.

JOHN 16:24, 33 PREVIOUSLY HAVE YOU ASKED NOTHING IN MY NAME; ASK, AND YOU SHALL RECEIVE, THAT YOUR JOY MAY BE FULL....THESE THINGS I HAVE SPOKEN UNTO YOU, THAT IN ME YOU MIGHT HAVE PEACE. IN THE WORLD YOU SHALL HAVE TRIBULATION; BUT BE OF GOOD CHEER; I HAVE OVERCOME THE WORLD.

<u>PHILIPPIANS 4: 19</u> MY GOD SHALL SUPPLY ALL MY NEED ACCORDING TO HIS RICHES IN GLORY, BY CHRIST JESUS.

<u>ROMANS 8:11, 26</u> BUT IF THE SPIRIT OF HIM THAT RAISED UP JESUS FROM THE DEAD DWELL IN YOU, HE THAT RAISED UP CHRIST FROM THE DEAD SHALL ALSO QUICKEN YOUR MORTAL BODIES BY HIS SPIRIT THAT DWELLS IN YOU. LIKEWISE THE SPIRIT ALSO HELPS OUR INFIRMITIES; FOR WE KNOW NOT WHAT WE SHOULD PRAY FOR AS WE OUGHT; BUT THE SPIRIT ITSELF MAKES INTERCESSION FOR US WITH GROANINGS WHICH CANNOT BE UTTERED.

<u>PSALM 46:1</u> GOD IS OUR REFUGE AND STRENGTH, A VERY PRESENT HELP IN TROUBLE.

<u>PHILIPPIANS 2:13</u> FOR IT IS GOD THAT WORKS IN YOU, BOTH TO WILL AND TO DO HIS GOOD PLEASURE.

<u>HEBREWS 10:23. 35</u> LET US HOLD FAST THE PROFESSION OF OUR FAITH WITHOUT WAVERING; (FOR HE IS FAITHFUL THAT PROMISED) CAST NOT AWAY THEREFORE YOUR CONFIDENCE, WHICH HAS GREAT RECOMPENSE OF REWARD.

<u>HEBREWS 11:1, 6</u> NOW FAITH IS THE SUBSTANCE OF THINGS HOPED FOR, THE EVIDENCE OF THINGS NOT SEEN. BUT WITHOUT FAITH IT IS IMPOSSIBLE TO PLEASE HIM; FOR HE THAT COMES TO GOD MUST BELIEVE THAT HE IS, AND THAT HE IS A REWARDER OF THEM THAT DILIGENTLY SEEK HIM.

<u>HEBREWS 13:8, 15-16</u> JESUS CHRIST, THE SAME YESTERDAY, AND TODAY, AND FOREVER. BY HIM THEREFORE LET US OFFER THE SACRIFICE OF PRAISE TO GOD CONTINUALLY, THAT IS THE FRUIT OF OUR LIPS, GIVING THANKS TO HIS NAME. BUT TO DO GOOD AND TO COMMUNICATE FORGET NOT, FOR WITH SUCH SACRIFICES GOD IS WELL PLEASED.

<u>2 CORINTHIANS 10:3-5</u> FOR THOUGH WE WALK IN THE FLESH, WE DO NOT WAR AFTER THE FLESH; FOR THE WEAPONS OF OUR WARFARE ARE NOT CARNAL, BUT MIGHTY THROUGH GOD TO THE PULLING DOWN OF STRONGHOLDS; CASTING DOWN IMAGINATIONS, AND EVERY HIGH THING THAT EXALTS ITSELF AGAINST THE KNOWLEDGE OF GOD, AND BRINGING INTO CAPTIVITY EVERY THOUGHT TO THE OBEDIENCE OF CHRIST.

<u>JAMES 5:14-16</u> IS ANY SICK AMONG YOU? LET HIM CALL FOR THE ELDERS OF THE CHURCH, AND LET THEM PRAY OVER HIM, ANOINTING HIM WITH OIL, IN THE NAME OF THE LORD, AND THE PRAYER OF FAITH SHALL SAVE THE SICK AND THE LORD SHALL RAISE HIM UP; AND IF HE HAVE COMMITTED SINS, THEY SHALL BE FORGIVEN HIM. CONFESS YOUR FAULTS ONE TO ANOTHER, AND PRAY ONE FOR ANOTHER, THAT YOU MAY BE HEALED. THE EFFECTUAL FERVENT PRAYER OF A RIGHTEOUS MAN AVAILS MUCH.

<u>1 PETER 2:24</u> (JESUS) WHO HIS OWN SELF BARE OUR SINS IN HIS OWN BODY ON THE TREE, THAT WE, BEING DEAD TO SINS, SHOULD LIVE TO RIGHTEOUSNESS; BY WHOSE STRIPES YOU WERE HEALED.

<u>1 JOHN 5: 4, 14-15</u> FOR WHATSOEVER IS BORN OF GOD OVERCOMES THE WORLD; AND THIS IS THE VICTORY THAT OVERCOMES THE WORLD, EVEN OUR FAITH. AND THIS IS THE CONFIDENCE THAT WE HAVE IN HIM, THAT IF WE ASK ANYTHING ACCORDING TO HIS WILL HE HEARS US. AND IF WE KNOW THAT HE HEAR US WHATSOEVER WE ASK, WE KNOW THAT WE HAVE THE PETITIONS THAT WE DESIRED OF HIM.

111 JOHN 1:2 BELOVED, I WISH ABOVE ALL THINGS THAT YOU MAY PROSPER AND BE IN HEALTH, EVEN AS YOUR SOUL PROSPERS.

JOHN 16:33 IN THE WORLD YOU SHALL HAVE TRIBULATION; BUT BE OF GOOD CHEER, I HAVE OVERCOME THE WORLD.

2 CHRONICLES 25:8-9 GOD HAS POWER TO HELP AND TO CAST DOWN. THE LORD IS ABLE TO GIVE YOU MUCH MORE THAN THIS.

2 CHRONICLES 26:5 AS LONG AS HE SOUGHT THE LORD, GOD MADE HIM TO PROSPER.

PSALM 103:5 (GOD) SATISFIES MY MOUTH WITH GOOD THINGS SO THAT MY YOUTH IS RENEWED LIKE THE EAGLE'S.

RUTH 4:15 (GOD) MAY HE BE TO YOU A RESTORER OF LIFE AND A NOURISHER AND SUPPORTER IN YOUR OLD AGE.

ISAIAH 54:14 IN RIGHTEOUSNESS SHALL YOU ESTABLISH; YOU SHALL BE FAR FROM OPPRESSION; FOR YOU SHALL NOT FEAR; AND FROM TERROR; FOR IT SHALL NOT COME NEAR YOU.

THANK YOU HEAVENLY FATHER THAT THE HEALING POWER AND WORD OF GOD IS WORKING MIGHTILY IN ME DRIVING OUT

SICKNESS AND DISEASE, ACHES AND PAINS, RESTORING AND CREATING MIRACLES IN MY BODY. I CHOOSE TO BELIEVE GOD AND HIS WORD.

IF YOU DO NOT KNOW JESUS AS THE SAVIOR OF YOUR LIFE, WE ENCOURAGE TO MEET HIM RIGHT NOW SO THAT YOU MAY BE RENEWED SPIRITUALLY AND BECOME PART OF GOD'S FAMILY. IF YOU'RE UNSURE WHETHER OR NOT YOU KNOW JESUS … THEN YOU DON'T KNOW HIM. PRAY NOW:

SALVATION PRAYER

JESUS, I CAN SEE THAT THERE'S SOMETHING MORE I NEED IN MY LIFE. THAT SOMETHING IS YOU I BELIEVE IN YOU, THAT YOU ARE THE SON OF GOD AND THAT YOU CAME TO EARTH AND DIED FOR MY SINS, AND THAT GOD RAISED YOU FROM THE DEAD. I'VE TRIED TO LIVE MY LIFE RIGHT, BUT I HAVEN'T ALWAYS DONE IT. PLEASE COME INTO MY LIFE. BE MY SAVIOR. HELP ME TO BE WHAT YOU WANT ME TO BE. AND NOW, AS I HAVE BEEN FORGIVEN, I NOW FORGIVE ANYONE WHO HAS EVER HURT ME, USED ME OR ABUSED ME. I RELEASE THEM, AND LET THEM GO. THANK YOU JESUS. I AM SAVED!

PRAYER AND DECLARATION FOR HEALING

FATHER I THANK YOU FOR YOUR WORD; THAT YOUR WORD WILL NOT RETURN TO YOU VOID, THAT YOUR WORD IS TRUE AND ANOINTED. THANK YOU MY FATHER, MY LORD AND MY GREAT GOD. THANK YOU HOLY SPIRIT. I EXPECT TO RECEIVE THE MANIFESTATION OF HEALING IN MY BODY. LORD JESUS, I WORSHIP YOU AND PRAISE YOU. IN JESUS' NAME, FATHER GOD, I PRAISE YOU, FOR THE LIFE IN MY LIMBS, EVERY JOINT, SOCKET, BONE, ORGAN, ARTERY, VEIN, BLOOD, TISSUE, MUSCLE, VALVE, TENDON, DISC, LIGAMENT, VERTEBRAE, CARTILAGE, NERVE, CELL, EVERYTHING IN MY BODY, THAT IT FUNCTION THE WAY GOD CREATED IT TO FUNCTION. (FOR GOOD HEALTH, TOUCH THE PITUITARY GLAND AT THE CENTER OF YOUR FOREHEAD AT HAIR LINE AND COMMAND THIS GLAND TO BE IN PERFECT WORKING ORDER. I COMMAND EVERY ELECTRICAL AND CHEMICAL FREQUENCY IN EVERY CELL OF MY BODY TO BE IN HARMONY AND BALANCE, AND TO DIGEST ALL THE BAD CELLS, IN JESUS' NAME. THANK YOU JESUS.) I PRAISE GOD FOR THE HOLY SPIRIT SENT TO BE MY WISDOM AND KNOWLEDGE, FOR MY UNDERSTANDING TO ALL THINGS. IN JESUS' NAME, I PRAISE GOD FOR _____

(SPEAK TO YOUR MOUNTAIN. COMMAND IT TO LEAVE, IN THE NAME OF JESUS CHRIST OF NAZARETH, BY THE POWER OF HIS SHED BLOOD AND THE MINISTRY AND POWER OF THE HOLY SPIRIT.) IN JESUS' NAME, AMEN.

The Healing Scriptures found here are available in Spanish. You may receive them by contacting me.

PROTECTION SCRIPTURES/ "FEAR NOT"

"Praying the actual scriptures is one of the most powerful things you can ever learn in life." John Bevere

Praise God for who He is until all fear is gone.
We can't be in faith, which pleases and reaches God, and fear at the same time. We all learned this in school. Two objects cannot occupy the same space at the same time. This is true in the natural and in the supernatural rhelm.

We must refuse fear and claim the promises of God; thank Him for all He's done for you in the past—He's never failed you before and He's not going to fail you now!

The devil wants you to run scared. All we have to do is stand against him in the strength of our God. The Bible says submit yourselves to God. Resist the devil and he will flee from you. You don't even have to fight. All you have to do is resist him. Refuse to accept fear; refuse to accept doubt. All the negative stuff in life comes from the devil anyway. God is the one who fights our battles. Jesus has already defeated the devil. We're the body of Christ. Jesus is our Head. We're the body and the devil is already under our feet. Nothing under your feet can hurt you.

Proverbs 2:7, 8 He (God) is a shield to those who walk uprightly. He guards the paths of justice, and preserves the way of His saints.

1 Samuel 2:9 (God) He will guard the feet of His godly ones.

Psalm 66:9 (God) keeps our soul among the living, and does not allow our feet to be moved.

Proverbs 3:25, 26 Do not be afraid of sudden terror, nor of trouble from the wicked when it comes, for the Lord will be your confidence, and will keep your foot from being caught.

2 Chronicles 16:9 For the eyes of the Lord run to and fro throughout the whole earth, to show Himself strong on behalf of those whose heart is loyal to Him.

Psalm 145:20 The Lord preserves all who love Him...

Psalm 91 He who dwells in the secret place of the Most High shall abide under the shadow of the Almighty. I will say of the Lord, "He is my refuge and my fortress; My God, in Him I will trust. Surely He shall deliver you from the snare of the fowler and from the perilous pestilence. He shall cover you with His feathers, and under His wings you shall take refuge; His truth shall be your (big) shield and buckler (small shield). You shall not be afraid of the terror by night, nor of the arrow that flies by day, nor of the pestilence that walks in darkness, nor of the destruction that lays waste at noonday. A thousand may fall at your side, and ten thousand at your right hand; but it shall not come near you. Only with your eyes shall you look and see the reward of the wicked. Because you have made the Lord, who is my refuge, even the Most High, your dwelling place, no evil shall befall you, nor shall any plague come near your dwelling; for He shall give His angels charge over you to keep you in all your ways. In their hands they shall bear you up, lest you dash your foot against a stone. You shall tread upon the lion and the cobra. The young lion and the serpent you shall trample underfoot. "Because he has set his love upon Me, therefore I will deliver him; I will set him on high, because he has known My name. He shall call upon Me, and I will answer him; I will be with him in trouble; I will deliver him and honor him. With long life I will satisfy him, and show him My salvation."

Luke 21:18 But not a hair of your head shall be lost.

Psalm 125:2 As the mountains surround Jerusalem, so the Lord surrounds His people...

Exodus 14:14 The Lord will fight for you, and you shall hold your peace.

2 Chronicles 32:8 ...with us is the Lord our God, to help us and to fight our battles.

Psalm 18:3/2 Samuel 22:4 I will call upon the Lord, who is worthy to be praised; so shall I be saved from my enemies.

Psalm 27:1 & 5 The Lord is my light and my salvation. Whom shall I fear or dread? The Lord is the Refuge and Stronghold of my life. Of whom shall I fear? For in the time of trouble He shall hide me in His pavilion; in the secret place of His tabernacle He shall hide me...

Psalm 31: 15, 20, 23 My times are in Your hands; delivering me from the hands of my foes and those who pursue me and persecute me. You shall hide them in the secret place of Your presence from the plots of men; You shall keep them secretly in a pavilion from the strife of tongues…The Lord preserves the faithful, and plentifully pays back him who deals haughtily.

Psalm 32:7 You are my hiding place; you shall preserve me from trouble; you shall surround me with songs of deliverance.

Psalm 18:30/Proverbs 30:5 He (God) is a shield to all who trust in Him.

Psalm 115:11 You who fear the Lord, trust in the Lord; He is their help and their shield.

Nahum 1:7 The Lord is good, a stronghold in the day of trouble; and He knows those who trust in Him.

Psalm 5:11 But let all those rejoice who put their trust in You; let them ever shout for You, because You defend them; let those also who love Your name be joyful in you.

Zechariah 9:16 The Lord their God will save them in that day, as the flock of His people, for they shall be like the jewels of a crown, lifted like a banner over His land.

Psalm 46:1 God is our refuge and strength, a very present help in trouble.

Proverbs 14:26 In the fear of the Lord there is strong confidence, and His children will have a place of refuge.

Proverbs 18:10 The Name of the Lord is a strong tower; the righteous run to it and are safe.

Isaiah 25:4 For you have been a strength to the poor, a strength to the needy in his distress, a refuge from the storm, a shade from the heat; for the blast of the terrible ones is as a storm against the wall.

Psalm 40:17/Psalm 70:5 But I am poor and needy; yet the Lord thinks upon me. You are my help and my deliverer. Do not delay, O my God.

1 Peter 5:7 ...casting all your care upon Him, for He cares for you.

Psalm 55:22 Cast your burden on the Lord, and He shall sustain you; He shall never permit the righteous to be moved.

Deuteronomy 33:27 The eternal God is your refuge, and underneath are the everlasting arms; He will thrust out the enemy from before you, and will say "Destroy!"

Proverbs 11:4 Riches do not profit in the day of wrath, but righteousness delivers from death

Proverbs 11:8 The righteous is delivered from trouble...

Proverbs 11:21 ...the posterity of the righteous will be delivered.

Proverbs 10:29 The way of the Lord is strength for the upright...

Proverbs 10:3 The Lord will not allow the righteous soul to famish...

Proverbs 10:6 Blessing are on the head of the righteous...

Proverbs 10:9 He who walks with integrity walks securely...

Proverbs 10:16 The labor of the righteous leads to life...

Proverbs 10:22 The blessing of the Lord makes one rich, and He adds no sorrow with it.

Proverbs 10:24 ...the desire of the righteous will be granted.

Proverbs 10:27-30 The fear of the Lord prolongs days...the hope of the righteous will be gladness...the way of the Lord is strength for the upright...the righteous will never be removed.

Proverbs 11:19 ...righteousness leads to life...

Proverbs 12:2 A good man obtains favor from the Lord...

Proverbs 12:13 ...the righteous will come through trouble.

Proverbs 12:21 No grave trouble will overtake the righteous...

Proverbs 14:26-27 In the fear of the Lord there is strong confidence, and His children will have a place of refuge. The fear of the Lord is a fountain of life, to turn one away from the snares of death.

Proverbs 30:5 Every word of God is pure; He is a shield to those who put their trust in Him.

Psalm 115:13 He will bless those who fear the Lord, both small and great.

Genesis 15:1 ...Fear not, I am your shield, and your exceeding great reward.

Genesis 26:24 ...Fear not, for I am with you, and will bless you...

Deuteronomy 20:3 & 4 ...Fear not...for the Lord your God is he that goes with you, to fight for you against your enemies, to save you.

Deuteronomy 31:6, 8 Be strong and of a good courage, fear not, nor be afraid of them: for the Lord your God, He it is that goes with you; He will not fail you, nor forsake you: fear not, neither be dismayed.

Joshua 8:1 ...Fear not, neither be dismayed...

Joshua 8:25 ...Fear not, nor be dismayed, be strong and of good courage; for shall the Lord do to all your enemies against whom you fight.

1 Chronicles 29:20 ...Be strong and of good courage, and do it; fear not, nor be dismayed: for the Lord God even my God, will be with you; He will not fail you, nor forsake you, until you have finished all the work for the service of the...Lord.

2 Chronicles 20:15 ...Thus said the Lord to you, Be not afraid nor dismayed by reason of this great multitude, for the battle is not yours, but God's.

2 Peter 2:9 The Lord knows how to deliver the godly out of temptations and trials.

Isaiah 35:4 Say to those who are of a fearful and hasty heart, Be strong, fear not! Behold your God will come with vengeance; with the recompense of God He will come and save you.

Isaiah 41:10 Fear not (there is nothing to fear), for I am with you; do not look around you in terror and be dismayed for I am your God. I will strengthen and harden you to difficulties. Yes, I will help you; yes I will hold you up and retain you with My (victorious) right hand of righteousness and justice.

Psalm 4:8 In peace I will both lie down and sleep, for You, Lord, alone make me dwell in safety and confident trust.

2 Peter 2:9 The Lord knows how to rescue the godly out of temptations and trials.

Isaiah 43:1-5 But now, thus says the Lord, He Who created you...and He who formed you...Fear not, for I have redeemed you; I have called you by your name; you are Mine. When you pass through the waters, I will be with you, and through the rivers, they will not overwhelm you. When you walk through the fire, you will not be burned or scorched, nor will the flame kindle upon you. For I am the Lord your God, the Holy One of Israel, your Savior...you are precious in My sight and honored...because I love you...Fear not for I am with you.

2 Thessalonians 3:3 ...The Lord is faithful, and He will strengthen and protect you from the evil one.

Proverbs 29:25 Fear of man will prove to be a snare, but whoever trusts in the Lord is kept safe.

Isaiah 44:2, 8 Thus says the Lord, Who made you and formed you from the womb...Fear not...Fear not nor be afraid in the coming violent upheavals.

Matthew 10:28 Do not be afraid of those who kill the body but cannot kill the soul; but rather be afraid of Him who can destroy both soul and body in hell (fear God).

Revelation 2:10 Fear nothing that you are about to suffer....Be loyally faithful unto death (even if you must die for it) and I will give you the crown of life.

Revelation 3:10, 11 Because you have guarded and kept My word of patient endurance. I also will keep you safe from the hour of trial (testing) which is coming on the whole world to try those who dwell upon the earth. Hold fast what you have...

Mark 13:3-37 Jesus tells us that we will hear of wars and rumors of wars, nation rising up against nation, famines and persecutions. He also tells us not be get frightened because all these things must happen in the last days.

Isaiah 54:14-15, 17 In righteousness shall you establish; you shall be far from oppression; for you shall not fear, and from terror, for it shall not come near you...whoever stirs up strife against you shall fall...But no weapon that is formed against you shall prosper and every tongue that shall rise against you in judgment you shall show to be in the wrong...

Psalm 118:6 The Lord is on my side. I <u>will not</u> fear. What can man do to me?

Hebrews 13:6 The Lord is my Helper. I <u>will not</u> be seized with alarm. (I will not fear or dread or be terrified).

2 Timothy 1:7 For God did not give us a spirit of timidity (of cowardice, of craven and cringing and fawning fear), but (He has given us a spirit) of power and of love and of clam and well-balanced mind and discipline and self control.

Isaiah 59:19 ...When the enemy shall come in, (comma placed differently) LIKE A FLOOD (emphasis placed here), the Spirit of the Lord shall lift up a standard against him.

Psalm 34:4, 7 & 8, 15, 17, 19 I sought the Lord and required Him and He heard me, and delivered me from all my fears...The Angel of the Lord encamps around those who fear Him and each of them He delivers. O taste and see that the Lord is good! Blessed is the man (and woman) who trusts and takes refuge in Him...When the righteous cry for help the Lord hears, and delivers them out of all their distress and troubles...Many evils confront the righteous, but the Lord delivers him out of them all.

Psalm 16: 1, 8 & 9 Keep and protect me, O God, for in You I have found refuge, and in You do I put my trust and hide myself...I have set the Lord continually before me; because He is at my right hand, I shall not be moved. Therefore, my heart is glad and my glory rejoices; my body too shall rest and confidently dwell in safety.

Isaiah 49:25 For thus says the Lord: Even the captives of the mighty will be taken away, and the prey of the terrible will be delivered; for I will contend with him who contends with you and I will give safety to your children and ease them.

Psalm 37:39-40 The salvation of the righteous is the Lord. He is their Refuge and secure Stronghold in the time of trouble, and the Lord helps them and delivers them. He delivers them from the wicked and saves them because they trust and take refuge in Him.

Joel 2: 32/Acts 2:21/Romans 10:13 ...And whoever shall call on the name of the Lord shall be delivered and saved.

Psalm 94:12, 13 & 19 Blessed is the man (or woman) whom You discipline and instruct O Lord, and teach out of Your law, that you may give him (her) power to keep himself (herself) calm in the days of adversity...in the multitude of my anxious thoughts within me, Your comforts cheer and delight my soul.

Philippians 1:27 & 28 ...conduct yourselves (that) your manner of life (will be) worthy of the good news (the Gospel) of Christ...and do not (for a moment) be frightened or intimidated in anything by your opponents and adversaries...

Philippians 4: 6 & 7 Do not fret or have any anxiety about anything but in every circumstance and in everything by prayer and petition, with thanksgiving, continue to make your wants know to God and God's peace shall be yours...that peace which transcends all understanding shall garrison and mount guard over your hearts and minds in Christ Jesus.

Psalm 3:3 But You O Lord, are a shield for me, my glory and the lifter of my head.

When things look hopeless, turn to God. He's the only One with the answer to all our troubles. He's already got your back covered. We have nothing to fear if we walk in His ways.

CPSIA information can be obtained at www.ICGtesting.com
Printed in the USA
LVOW13s0707271013

358725LV00001B/46/P

9 781606 476864